ORSON WELLES
JOURNEY OF A FILMMAKER

BY CHRIS WADE

ORSON WELLES: JOURNEY OF A FILMMAKER
Wisdom Twins Books, 2018
wisdomtwinsbooks.weebly.com

This edition released in 2018

Text Copyright of Chris Wade, 2018

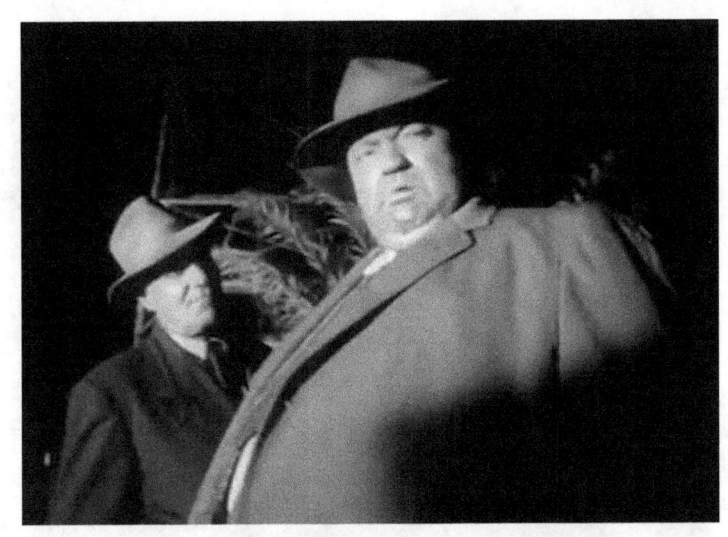

ORSON WELLES
JOURNEY OF A FILMMAKER

CHRIS WADE

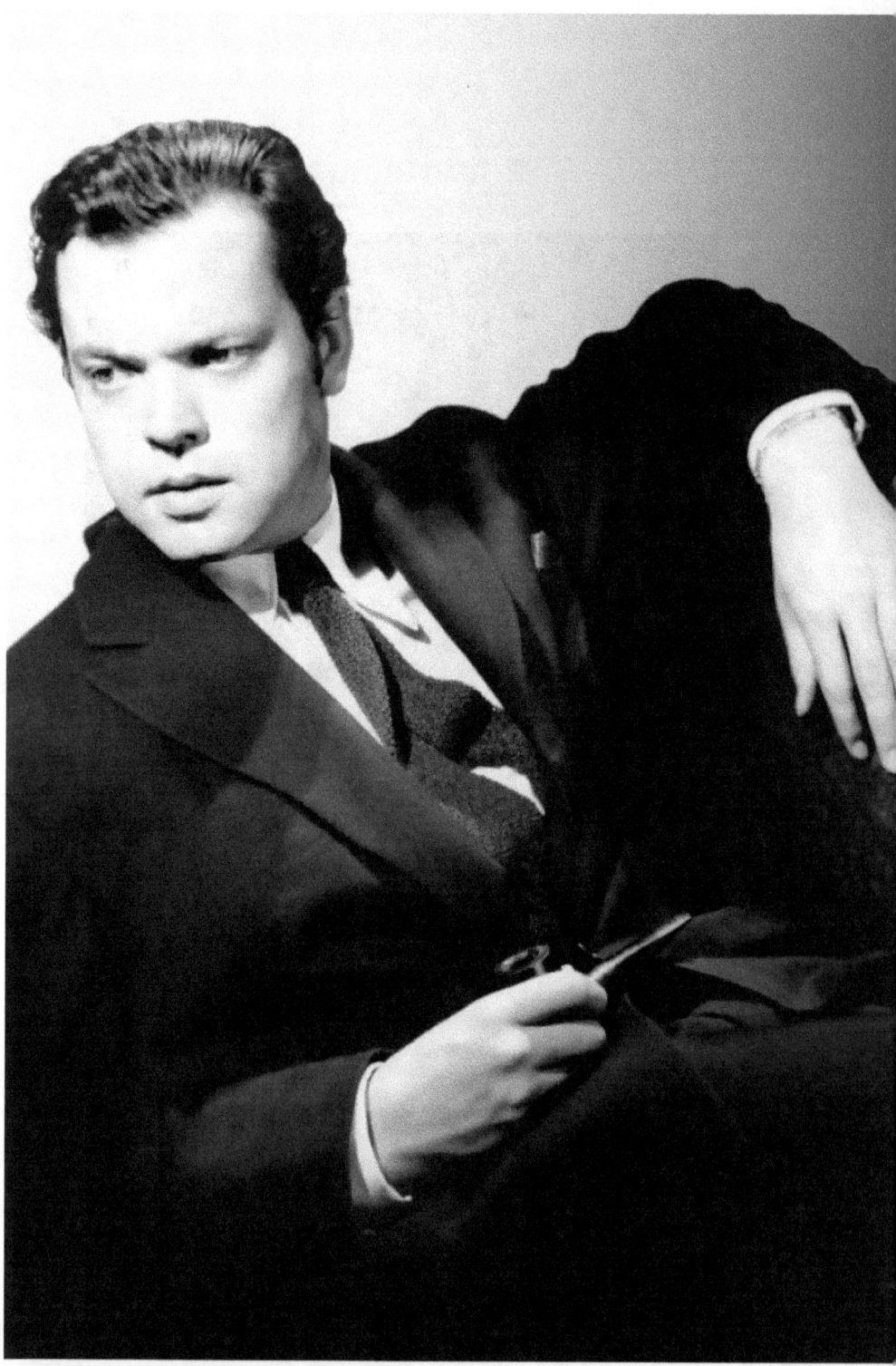

CONTENTS

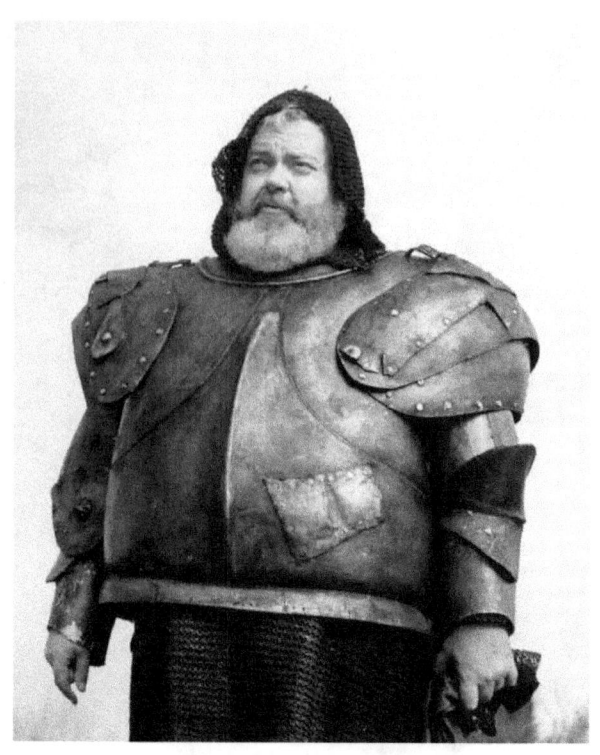

INTRODUCTION

Orson Welles, the pioneer of maverick filmmaking, began his directorial career at the age of 26 when he wrote, produced, starred in and directed Citizen Kane in 1941, a movie still cited to be the greatest ever made. Though he struggled to regain the kind of control he had with his debut on subsequent films, Welles achieved more than most directors and made some remarkable masterpieces along the way, such as The Magnificent Ambersons, Chimes At Midnight and the singular F For Fake. The most remarkable thing about Welles' long, varied and winding career as a director though, is the fact that it ended, finally it seems, thirty three years after his death, with the recent release of the Netflix funded The Other Side of the Wind.

For some, myself included, the debut and the posthumous finale are almost like two sides of the same coin, at least in terms of stylistic content and historical importance. Both are stunning in their respective technical wizardry, enigmatic in their exploration of their central characters, wonderfully subversive, and hugely intimidating in their fierce intelligence. Both are about two magnetic yet mysterious men who harbour secrets and complexities not clear to the outside eye. Though perhaps a simplistic theory, Charles Foster Kane and Jake Hannaford could be seen as twin alter egos for Orson Welles. Admittedly, Welles did say that Hannaford had no autobiographical elements whatsoever, and was an invention, a parody of a macho filmmaker, but the cloaked mystery of Hannaford, and more so Kane, are simplified extensions of Welles' most legendary traits. Both films are mysteries wrapped up in layers of enigma, and that could also be said of Welles. Orson was part illusionist (he was a magician after all), part genius, part hoodwinker and one hundred percent a creator of self myth. "I hate anything that's become folkloric," he once said, rather ironically. Perhaps he was unaware that in his own life time he had become a myth himself. Then again, perhaps not.

"Citizen Kane is the greatest curse of my life," he said in one interview. If Kane was the curse, then The Other Side of the Wind, now here in existence, finally, for us all to feast upon, is the posthumous cure. Of course, Welles is not here anymore and cannot see the fruits of his labour becoming a reality that is both enthralling and true to his legacy, but there is a final irony in the fact that the film he tried so hard to complete with his own money, saw entangled in legal fees and ultimately scrapped is now available to anyone with a viewing screen in their home. He'd be pleased, no doubt.

It may trigger off a rolling of the eyes, but I do see The Other Side of the Wind as the eventual reply to Kane. Welles once said Hollywood viewed him as a kind of ghost of Christmas future, a bearded beatnik who foresaw the change in the studio system and the role of the filmmaker. The freedom he gained on that film spelled the death of his freedom thereafter, at least within the Hollywood grinding machine. Kane had haunted Welles forever, and like the shackles of some tormented spook, his myth was tied to that movie until his death and beyond. Now, though dead, Welles has made a movie that not only equals Kane in terms of enigma, technical invention and thought provoking power, but becomes an essential postscript to it. After all, the film's focal point, Hannaford, is a man whose past is rich, but his present and future less impressive to the ass kissers, leaches and hangers-on who follow him relentlessly, cameras in hand, through the swirling chaos of his 70th birthday party. Welles suffered a similar fate, forever hounded by film students, critics and cineastes who proclaimed him a genius one minute and a has-been chancer the next. The Other Side of the Wind not only feels like a self conscious examination of his own life, filtered through a boozy, safari suited, ultra macho protagonist, but a final joke, a last punch to the gut of a Hollywood that had no time for the man who revolutionised the movie business.

To me, the Welles tale now feels, if not fully completed, then at least rounded off. While there are still loose ends, mysteries and abandoned film projects forever residing in storage facilities, that great final statement, The Other Side of the Wind, is now out there, and it's as faithful to Welles' original aims as it's possible to be. While only a few years ago Welles' tale was a romanticised ballad of a maverick genius abused by the studios and robbed of the chance to fulfil his brilliance, it is now a knowing, defiant and biting story that begins and ends with two marvellous masterpieces, the first a naive, wide eyed vision of a dreamer, the latter a conscious declaration of independence and prickly rebellion from a bruised and battered veteran. This book explores the beginning, middle and end of Orson's career as a director, focusing on the miraculous Citizen Kane at the start and the cyclonic The Other Side of the Wind at the finale. Both are films of betrayal, magic, identity and labyrinthine puzzles, and are perhaps his two most seminal works, if mostly in conjunction with Welles legend. This is, in some respects, the ending we have been waiting for; and though not a perfectly, tidy and ordered finish, it's a typically Wellesian conundrum of a final curtain.

(NOTE: This book features some material from my previous book on Welles, to provide focus to the new points made.)

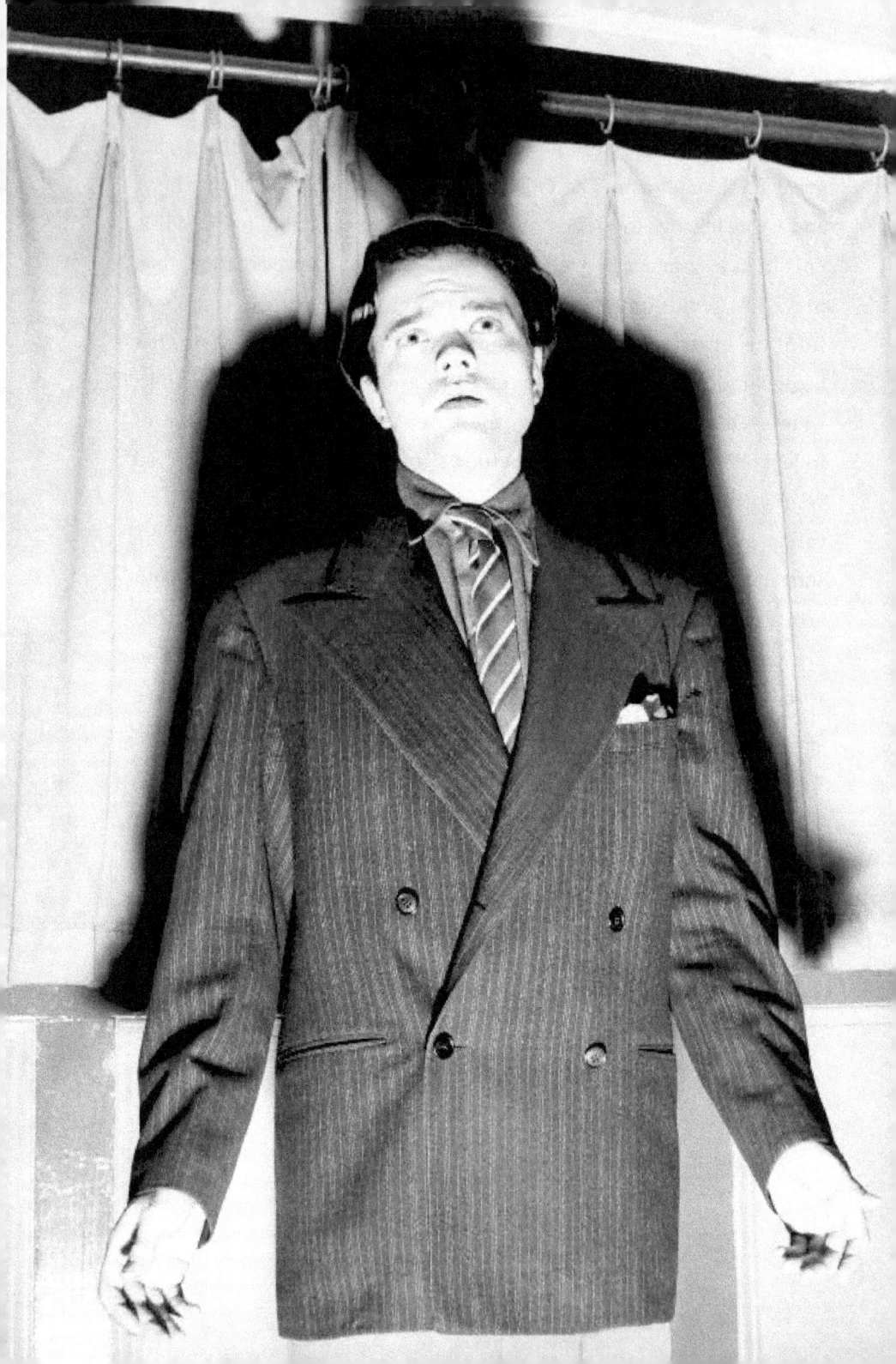

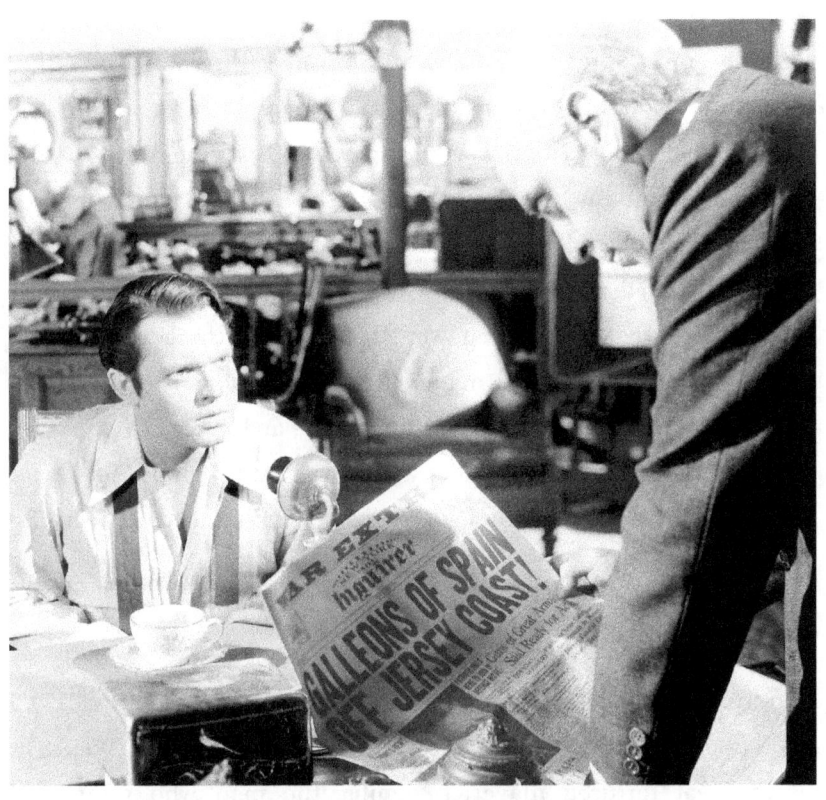

JOURNEY OF A FILMMAKER
From Citizen Kane to The Other Side of the Wind

When looking at the directorial work of Orson Welles, and the masterpieces within it, it is important to remember that he abandoned or was unable to complete just as many films as he finished and released to the public. The world knows him for Citizen Kane, that dazzling 1941 masterpiece, in which he starred and directed, but there a host of obscure, unfinished, lost and plain baffling film projects that never saw the light of day. For quite some time, the most legendary of these unfinished films was The Other Side of the Wind, his ambitious semi autobiographical passion project which he began in 1970, worked on sporadically through the 70s and 80s, and eventually abandoned when the required funds proved impossible to obtain. Orson Welles died in 1985, and the film was never completed. He did, however, say to filmmaker and friend Peter Bogdanovich that if anything were to happen to him, Peter would promise to get the movie made. It's a remarkable feat then, that nearly fifty years after he started making it, and over 33 years since his death (Orson would be 103 now if he were still living), The Other Side of the Wind has finally been released. And with the unleashing of this mythical film, Orson's directorial career has been bookended. It begins with Kane and ends 76 years later with this Netflix funded mythical movie. And that is what this essay is about.

In my previous book on Welles (The Final Cut, released in 2017), I wrote a piece on the clichéd and over romanticised idea of Welles as film's great tortured maverick genius, the man who reinvented cinema with Citizen Kane and then suffered a slow decline, where every film that followed failed to measure up to his debut and he was forced to take acting jobs in ropey films to fund his passion projects. Welles is often referred to as film's great tragedy, the wunderkind genius who never fulfilled that early promise. What many people choose to overlook though is the fact that Citizen Kane is not necessarily the pinnacle of his directing career. Just because critics have said so for some seventy odd years does not make it necessarily true. In a funny way, Citizen Kane really is the" greatest picture ever made" (it's been called this for decades now), but perversely, for me at least, it is not his finest picture. If you view Kane as the best film of all time, naturally anything that follows will be a let down. However, Welles' biggest mistake according to the system was not repeating himself. Sure, he could have made something as dynamic and arresting immediately upon its release, but he chose to venture into other areas.

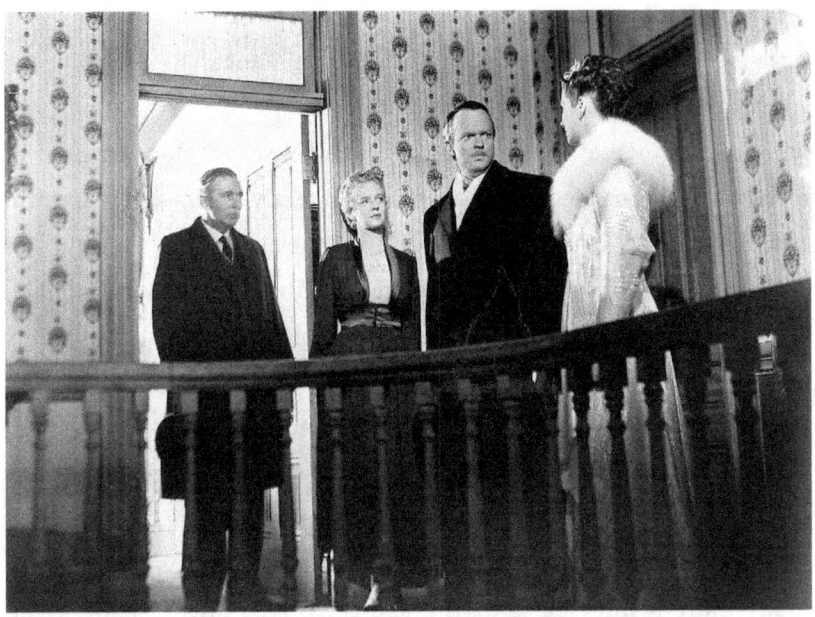

A scene from Citizen Kane

His follow up film came a year later in 1942, The Magnificent Ambersons, a beautiful but down beat film taken from his grasp and cut to within an inch of its life. Welles said they killed the film, and that in effect killed him. He was forever bruised, hurt and haunted by the film's treatment, but Welles would not stay down. A year later he was uncredited director on the less distinguished Journey Into Fear, and in 1946 he directed The Stranger, a fine picture which Orson himself did not rate very highly. After all, he was comparing it to Citizen Kane and what he was really capable of. They had given him final cut for Kane, but were reluctant to do so again. And that was all he wanted, the full control of his work. Was he really asking too much?

To say Welles never made a truly great picture again though is pure poppycock. The Lady from Shanghai, released in 1947, is a staggering enigma of a movie, crammed full of startling imagery and iconic cinematic moments (the mirror scene alone ensures it remains a masterpiece of its time). His early Shakespearean film adaptations are equally powerful, yet they were made on tight budgets as and when he had the money to film them. Macbeth (1948) remains one of the most powerful Shakespearean films of all time, and it was followed three years later by his version of Othello, which won the main prize at the Cannes Film Festival. Anyone who sits and seriously considers the latter two movies would have to admit they match Kane for visual power and poetic depth.

Welles only made two films in the 1950s as director (he acted in many more it must be said), the less celebrated Mr. Arkadin (1955) and the cinematic classic Touch of Evil (1958). The latter, an undeniable masterpiece on every level, should really have made things easier for Orson in Hollywood. Yet they still saw him as a maverick and refused to give him the kind of control and funds he needed to bring his vision to life. Today, Touch of Evil is like a blue print for high quality filmmaking, and even though it was a homage to an earlier era, it was way ahead of its time in terms of technicality.

He made similar advancement in 1962's The Trial, his adaptation of Franz Kafka's classic novel, but it was in Chimes At Midnight, Welles' tribute to Shakespeare's Falstaff, that Orson made a masterpiece so staggeringly good it would have taken over Kane's reign as the finest film ever made if it had received the same kind of exposure. As it was though, Chimes At Midnight didn't even see a US release. Again, Welles' genius went unrecognised.

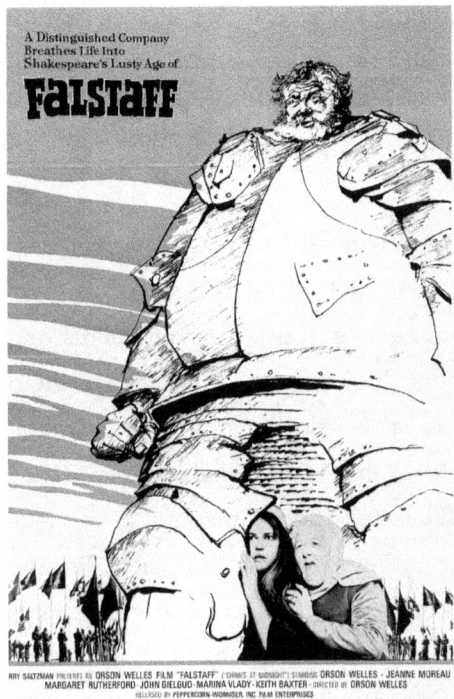

The poster for Welles' Chimes At Midnight.

It's easy to get wrapped up in the romanticised myth of Welles as the great tragic casualty of Hollywood, but a serious look at his filmography, especially the latter part, reveals many artistic successes., Granted, dream projects were abandoned and he still had to appear in movies undeserving of his status for cash, but his later directorial works are as important as Kane.

The Immortal Story, released in 1968, was adapted from Karen Blixen's story. It remains one of Welles' most measured, calm and haunting works, low on technical wizardry but oozing atmosphere and tragic beauty. It could not have been more different to the final film he directed in his life time (or at least the last one he saw released), the chaotic, swirling majesty of 1974's F For Fake. A film essay about forgery and lies, Welles weaved a contradictory web of labyrinthine paradoxes and illusions which went over many people's heads at the time, but is today seen as one of his essential masterworks.

Many Welles aficionados, myself included, like to dwell in the "lost" category, his unfinished dream films, and though it may at first seem to be an unrewarding area to obsess over, it is a place of wonder and mystery. What is so enticing about these movies, or the idea of them at least, is that the footage that exists is so unusual, so free and often so surreal that the fragments take on a new air of mystery. These films were doomed from the off set and, indeed, may not have made masterpieces of themselves even if they had been completed. But the crackly snapshots we have are so tempting, and so frustrating, that it becomes impossible not to wallow in the realm of the "could have beens", of which there are many in Welles' career as a director.

The Other Side of the Wind was not his only great obsession. One of his most fabled abandoned pictures was Don Quixote, the dream picture for many a filmmaker, which he worked on from 1957 onwards, in various guises and concepts. Initially a 30 minute TV special proposal, Orson wanted to bring Quixote and his right hand man Sancho Panza into the modern age. For Welles, it wasn't so much the story itself but what the men in that epic tale meant to him.

"My Don Quixote and Sancho Panza are exactly and traditionally drawn from Cervantes, but are nonetheless contemporary. What interests me is the idea of these dated old virtues. And why they still seem to speak to us when, by all logic, they're so hopelessly irrelevant. That's why I've been obsessed for so long with Don Quixote... He can't ever be contemporary—that's really the idea. He never was. But he's alive somehow, and he's riding through Spain even now. The anachronism of Don Quixote's knightly armour in what was Cervantes' own modern time doesn't show up very sharply now. I've simply translated the anachronism. My film demonstrates that he and Sancho Panza are eternal."

In the final statement, Welles could have been talking about himself. However, this vision never came to fruition, and Welles tried again and again to get it going. In the 1970s, he and Gary Graver attempted to bring it to the screen, and even by the 1980s, he decided it could work as an essay film in the style of F For Fake. Again, it all came to nothing.

His legendary lost films The Deep and The Heroine were his most well known abandoned projects of the 1960s, films which either collapsed through lack of funding, or in the case of the very promising looking The Deep, because the lead actor died. (Laurence Harvey died in 1973, and Welles ceased the production for good.) The Deep was actually a conscious effort on Welles' part to go commercial. "My hope is that it won't be an art-house movie," Orson said at the time. "I hope it's the kind of movie I enjoy seeing myself. I felt it was high time to show that we could make some money."

Unfortunately, The Deep was another film which never came to light. Surviving footage promised a classic, which makes it all the more frustrating. But there are other lesser written of projects too. One of the best of these is undoubtedly One Man Band, also known as Orson Welles' London.

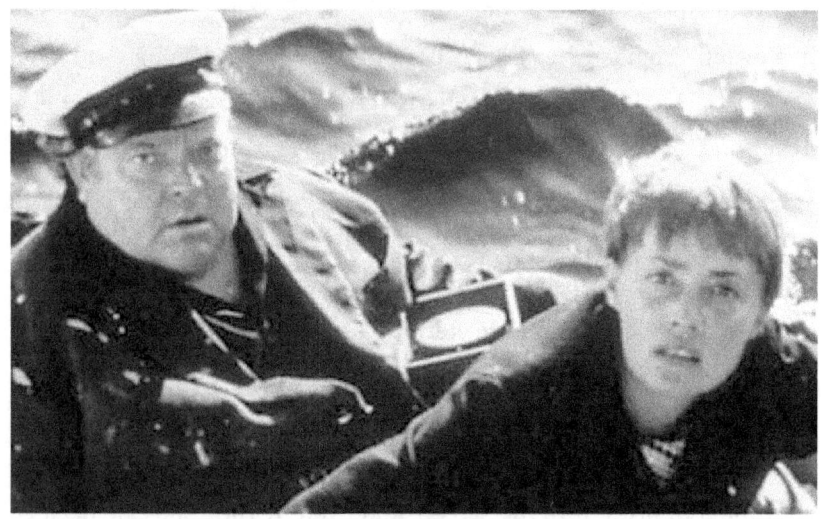

Welles' abandoned film, The Deep.

Tim Brooke Taylor is best known as one third of The Goodies - alongside Bill Oddie and Graeme Garden - the madcap 70s comic team watched by millions all over the UK every week. Tim is also known for his work in landmark TV shows like At Last the 1948 Show with John Cleese, and as a panellist on the ongoing I'm Sorry I Haven't A Clue radio show. One of the most obscure projects he was a part of, though only obscure because it was never released, was Orson Welles' brilliant One Man Band film. The movie is split into five segments, and Tim appears as a bowler hatted reporter in the

Swinging London section. Though not officially released, this segment can be viewed, in scratchy quality it must be added, online as part of the Lost Films of Orson Welles. It's surreal, mad, and absolutely unmissable.

"Graeme Garden and I made two series of a sketch show called Broaden Your Mind in 1968 and 69," Tim told me. "We were watching the first programme of the second series in Graeme's flat. As it ended Graeme's phone rang. He answered it, said a few words, put the phone down and said 'that was Orson Welles'. I remember saying 'What a coincidence, I was expecting a call from the Pope'.

"It *was* Orson. He'd seen some of the first series and got our phone numbers. We saw him the next day and agreed to write and shoot some stuff with him. Which we did. We were gobsmacked, but got on with him really well. The One Man Band Song was one of Bill Oddies's which we had included in one of our shows."

One cannot overlook the most intriguing of all the lost works, The Dreamers, which Welles began in 1979 with his girlfriend, muse and collaborator Oja Kodar. Based on the works of Karen Blixen, it was Henry Jaglom who attempted to get the film off the ground and attract funders. It was Hal Ashby who originally provided the forwarding fee needed for Orson to finish the script, but once he read the finished product (for want of a better word) he chose not to pursue it any closer.

At his own expense Welles shot some test teaser footage with Oja, using his home as a set. It was for a while a sort of fabled few minutes of footage, written about by the selected few who had seen it at small screenings or gatherings. With its inclusion in the Orson documentary One Man Band, the footage is now less obscure, and it has to be said, is absolutely brilliant. It has a simplicity about it, with Orson letting Oja provide her effortless charm while we see only the back of him, as enigmatic and mysterious as ever. It's low key, it's beautiful, and it's the only bit we have it. Unfortunately Orson never found funding for the film. Another lost opportunity.

Even when I wrote my previous book on Welles in 2017, it looked unlikely that The Other Side of the Wind would ever get released. Indeed, it seemed it would forever reside in the "lost films" category. But when Netflix came to the rescue, one of the most legendary and mythical unfinished movies of all time was finally going to see the light of day. Were any Welles fanatics secretly disappointed, worried even, that the film would finally be completed and perhaps not live up to the hype, the myth and the hope? This is the one Welles' reputation had been riding on, the film he had obsessively tried to get made and referred to most frequently in latter day interviews. In many ways, The Other Side of the Wind was going to be the bookend to Citizen Kane, the final instalment in one of the most remarkable and influential CVs in filmmaking history. And now, finally, the world at large can see Welles' final cinematic statement. They may not like what they see, nor understand it, but they can certainly admire what the big man had in mind.

In many ways, the release of The Other Side of the Wind is rather poetic, and it seems that Orson has had the last laugh. "They'll love me when I'm dead" he so famously apparently said; and it seems, whether he really said it or not, Welles was right.

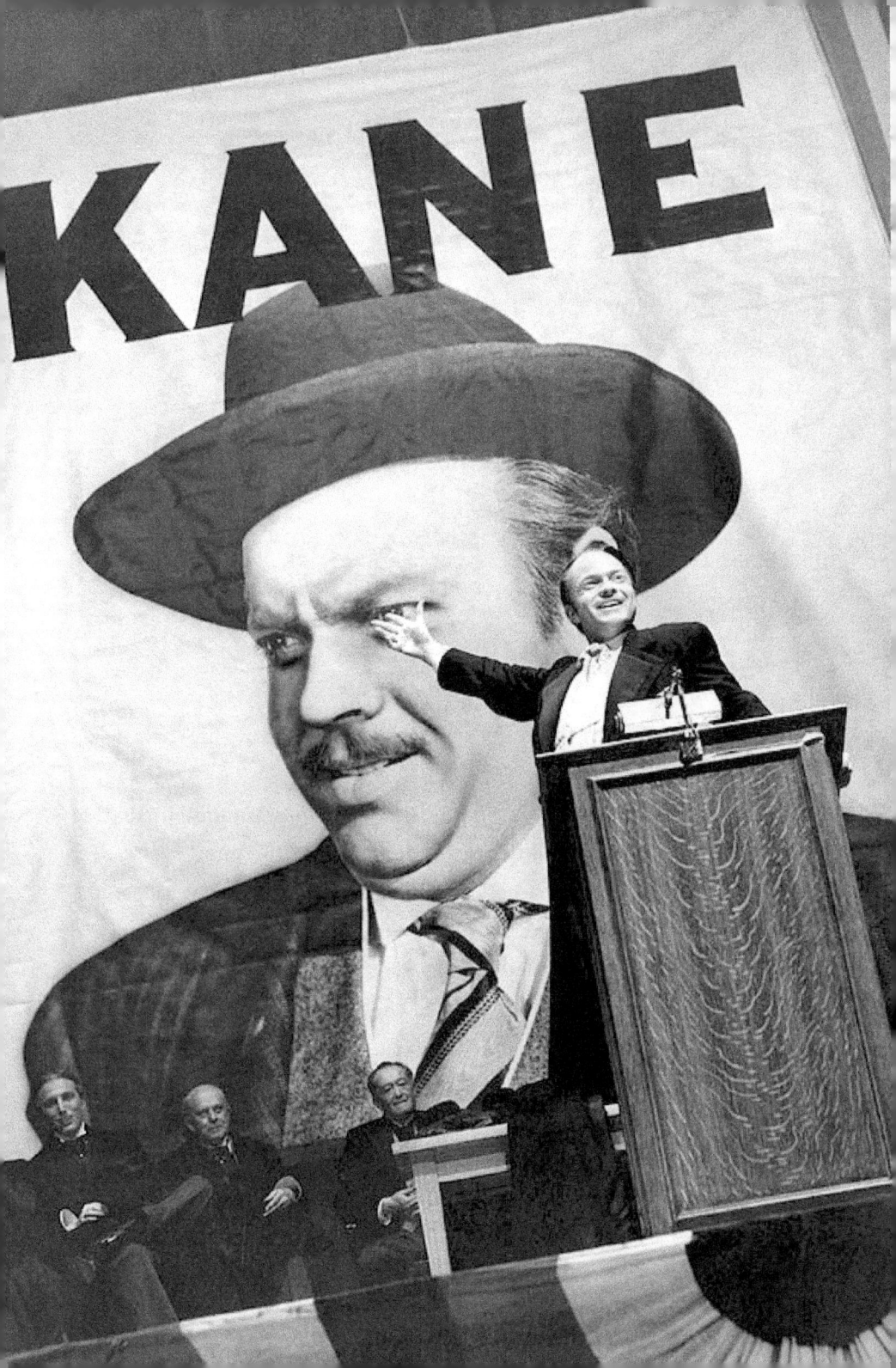

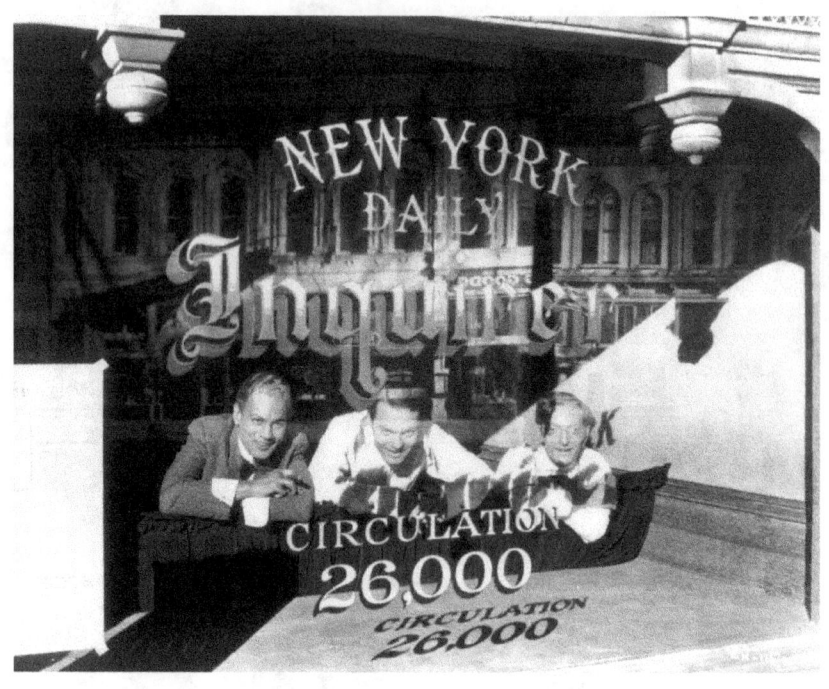

"I don't think any word can explain a man's life"

But we must rewind to make sense of this posthumous finale. For years Citizen Kane had the reputation of being the finest movie ever made, and certainly the best to come out of Hollywood. It topped the various film magazine critics' polls for decades, seemingly forever to be viewed as the pinnacle of filmmaking. Though some seemed to tire of Kane's continued scaling of the top ten, few could genuinely deny the film's mighty influence and innovative qualities. Wonderfully directed from the first image, it's a film which unravels like a great mystery, though one could argue the final layer never really comes off, ensuring the whole thing remains enigmatic and mythical, much like Welles himself. Every set up, every shot and every image is a work of art, and there are few films one can mention which match its sheer visual perfection.

When I was growing up, magazines would cite Kane as the zenith, the towering height of cinema, and proclaim that nothing could get close. As a boy, hooked on colourful fantasies and cartoons like all kids, it seemed to be this stuffy, unapproachable black and white movie from yesteryear. But of course as soon as I got to the right age and saw it, I was dazzled by its innovative structure, dizzying pace, the performances and the thrill of its vast array of visuals. I realised just why the critics kept selecting it as the greatest movie of all time.

Then there was a slight shift, but only very slight I might add. For years, Kane had stood at the top of the BFI's yearly best films ever made list, movies chosen by critics for their lasting power. Suddenly, in 2012's round up, Citizen Kane was knocked off by Alfred Hitchcock's worthy but nowhere near as influential or enjoyable Vertigo. It was a landmark moment, at least if you value critics and their opinions at all. Is this poll really reflective of Orson and Kane's popularity? Does it even matter?

"And the loser is – Citizen Kane," Ian Christie wrote, ridiculously I might add, in September 2012's Sight and Sound Magazine poll. "After 50 years at the top, Orson Welles's debut film has been convincingly ousted by Alfred Hitchcock's 45th feature Vertigo – and by a whopping 34 votes, compared with the mere five that separated them a decade ago. So what does it mean? Given that Kane actually clocked over three times as many votes this year as it did last time, it hasn't exactly been snubbed by the vastly larger number of voters taking part in this new poll, which has spread its net far wider than any of its six predecessors. But it does mean that Hitchcock, who only entered the top ten in 1982 (two years after his death), has risen steadily in esteem over the course of 30 years, with Vertigo climbing from seventh place, to fourth in 1992, second in 2002 and now first, to make him the Old Master. Welles, uniquely, had two films (The Magnificent Ambersons as well as Kane) in the list in 1972 and 1982, but now Ambersons has slipped to 81st place in the top 100. So does 2012 – the first poll to be conducted since the internet became almost certainly the main channel of communication about films – mark a revolution in taste?"

The answer to that question is, of course, no. Just because one poll puts Vertigo in front of Citizen Kane does not mean there has been a shift in tastes at all. Alternatively, just because critics have called it the best film ever made for decades doesn't mean Citizen Kane itself is necessarily so either. To a certain type of film viewer, perhaps of a certain age, Kane is an undoubtable masterpiece, but as the generations go on (and even though new directors will be influenced by it), most young filmgoers would prefer to watch a superhero climb up a skyscraper to save an endangered vixen than a complex, interwoven satirical study of a man named Kane.

Ironically, the one person who might have been secretly pleased that Kane slipped off the top spot was Welles himself. Just think about it, he was forever being reminded that Kane was the best cinema could get, thus rendering any pursuit he took afterwards pointless and bound for disappointment on some level. If other filmmakers viewed Kane as an intimidating masterwork when embarking on their own film projects (one would feel like a Sunday painter glancing across at the Mona Lisa), just imagine how much the grand old classic haunted Welles himself, a man ever so keen to prove he still had what it took to make a true classic, but was denied the chance to do so. From the early forties to his death in 1985, Welles had the strange displeasure of being told a film he made decades earlier while still in his mid twenties was the peak of film, and it was pointless trying to match it. No wonder he was so tortured by the odd road his career went down.

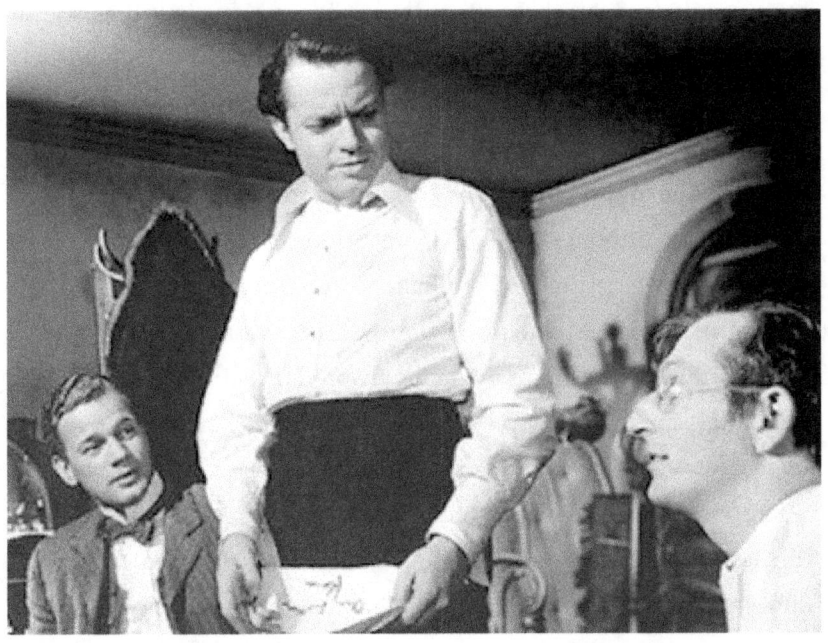

Welles in his masterpiece, Citizen Kane.

Though it's now 77 years old (at the time of writing), little or nothing about the movie has changed in all that time. It's still a blue print of how to direct a movie, a masterpiece of technique, montage, dissolve, voice over, performance and soundtrack. When you consider where movies were at in 1941, Kane's labyrinthine qualities seem to be even more breathtaking. Sure, Hollywood fare was solid, but most of it was unchallenging; romantic tales, quirky comedies, and shoot 'em up gangster pictures were the order of the day. Ten years before the arrival of Marlon Brando in A Streetcar Named Desire, a film and actor combo which unarguably changed movies as the world knew them, Orson Welles signalled the true arrival of a shift in stylistic concerns. Indeed, all these years later, Citizen Kane is still as stylish, sharp and swift as it ever was. When Orson said in a 1960 interview, "I didn't know that there were things you couldn't do, so anything I could think up in my dreams, I attempted to photograph," he came out with the most telling and complete statement about the film anyone ever uttered. Kane is a dream, and more than any movie before or since, it defines our hazy, complicated, and otherworldly visions of slumber, the projections of our restless mind. Welles' background in the theatre no doubt ensured the film had its powerful dramatic flair, and ensured scenes were framed majestically, as if seen on an elevated stage. It gives the film a certain grandness.

The movie business first had its eyes set on Welles in the mid thirties, but everything they sent to him for consideration was turned down flat. Clearly, nothing in the cinema could tempt Welles away from the vitality of the theatre. Welles was later adamant when speaking to his friend Gary Graver that he never got as excited about movies as he did the theatre, painting, or even bullfighting. That he also claimed to be in love with the filmmaking medium somewhat contradicts these claims, but one could say Welles definitely had a love-hate relationship with the cinema.

Looking at Welles' career at the time though, and before, it's simple to see why he wasn't so bothered about getting into the rigid world of filmmaking. The child prodigy had entered the world of theatre, firstly heading to Ireland with the inheritance from his father's death (his beloved mother had died when he was a small boy, meaning Orson was now an orphan without a spiritual home), living the life of a rag tag gypsy. He entered Dublin's Gate Theatre and pretended to be a noted actor in America, despite being only 16. Though they did not believe him, they were amused by Orson and admired his bravery, agreeing to give him stage work there. His debut was at the end of October in a production of Jew Suss. He continued to perform there until he moved on to the Abbey Theatre the following year for an adaptation of W. Somerset Maugham's the Circle. The boy genius, who could read at two and recite Shakespeare when other children were just grasping the alphabet, was finally making his way in the exciting world of live theatre.

When he returned to the USA he took on some writing work, and in 1933 began to get steady theatre work in New York. He worked tirelessly in 33, getting valuable experience and appearing in 200 performances throughout the year. It was in 1934 that he first entered the world of radio, a totally different medium in some ways but very similar in others. Like on stage, the radio welcomed exuberant acting, projected and heightened to reach the audience, in this case the listener, many of whom were tuning in from miles away across the USA. Though the stage was exciting to Orson, it also had its limitations. There was only so much you could do, given the size of the stage and budgetary constraints, but on the radio, as long as the listener had an imagination and was firmly along for the ride, almost anything could be achieved.

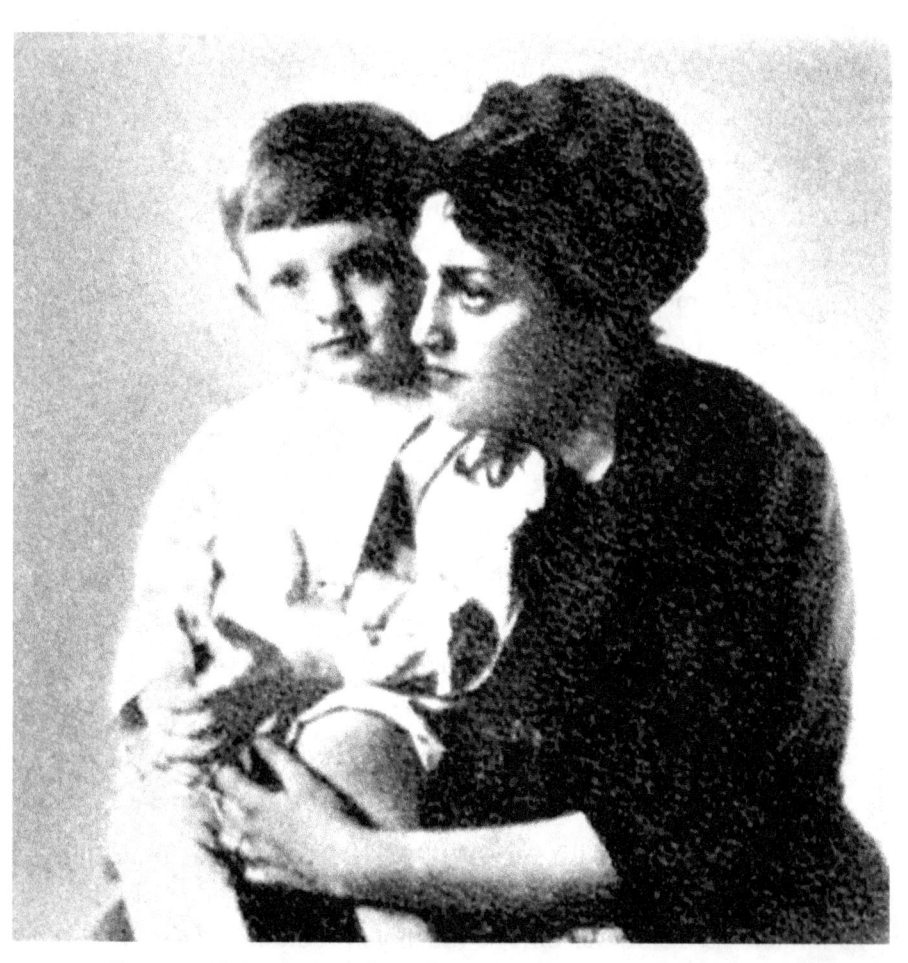

Orson with his beloved mother, who died when he was a child.

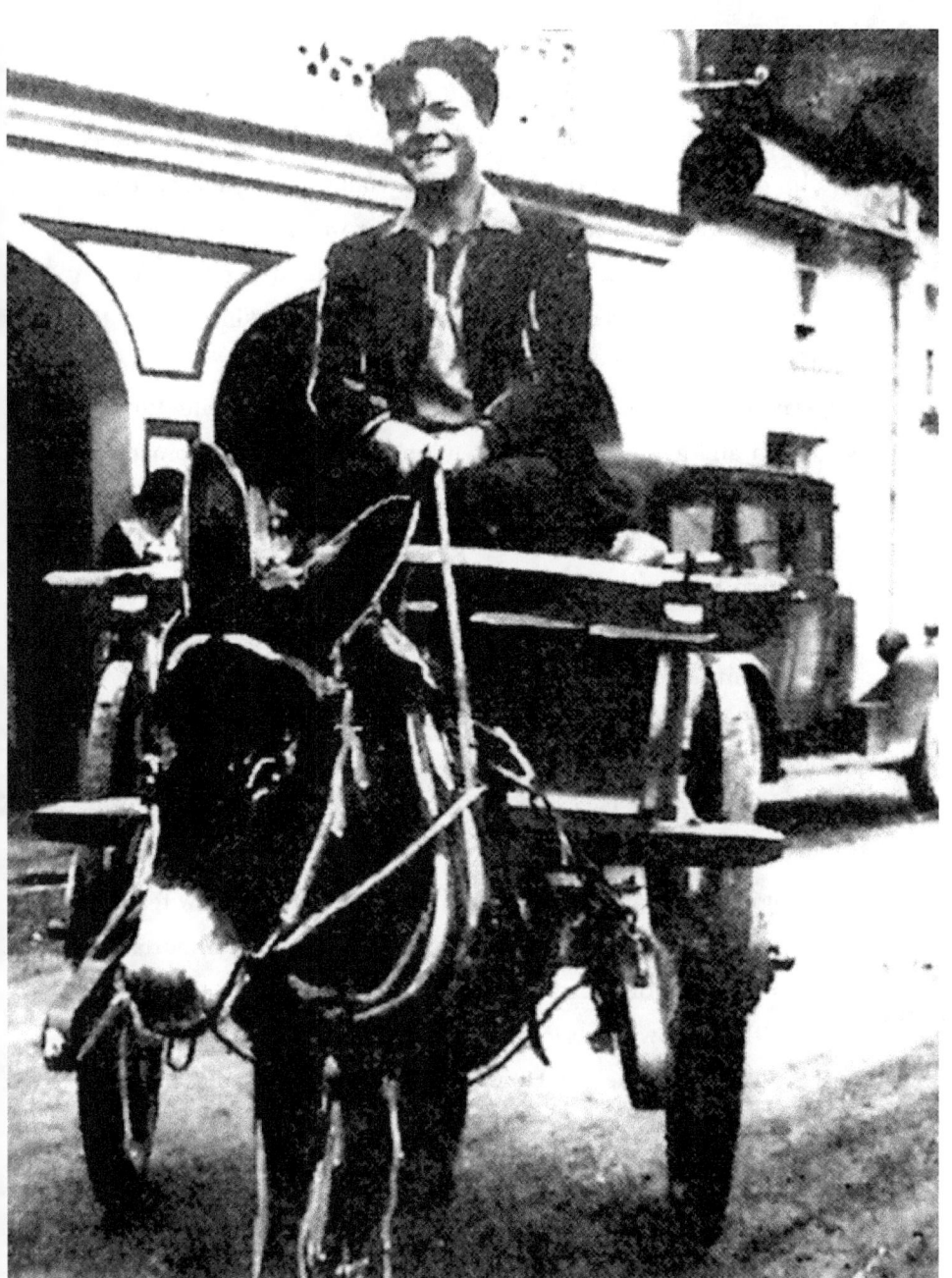

A Man of Myth; young Orson setting out on the road...

In 1934 he began to appear on the American School On Air, while also performing in Shakespeare on stage. The same year he filmed his film debut, the short but joyously entertaining The Hearts of Age. Welles later dismissed it as a minor amateur work, which indeed it is, but any Orson admirer should take out the time to watch it. True, it doesn't hint at his subsequent wizardry in the filmmaking field in the slightest, but it remains harmless naive fun.

It was a big time for Orson; he married his first wife Virginia Nicoloson and gained positive attention for his work in Romeo and Juliet in New York, where he was spotted by the theatre producer John Houseman. He cast Welles in a production of Panic, shortly after which he appeared on CBS radio reciting a speech from it. By now, the not yet twenty year old Welles was gaining a healthy income from radio and theatre.

"I was so employed I forgot how to sleep" is how Welles described his busy schedule for the next few years, working with Houseman in the Federal Theatre Project. Welles was making a killing on radio ($1,500 a week) and putting his wages into theatre productions. His 1936 staging of an all black Macbeth certainly ruffled a few feathers, but it was also an acclaimed production and mightily important in the development of racial acceptance. The production toured the States, with the now twenty year old Welles already being viewed as a genius. It was when he and Houseman founded the Mercury Theatre though, that things really stepped up a gear. He opened it at the end of 37 with a modernised version of Julius Caesar which went down a storm. Within a matter of months, Welles was on the cover of Time Magazine, credited for revolutionising the theatre, despite still being only 23.

30

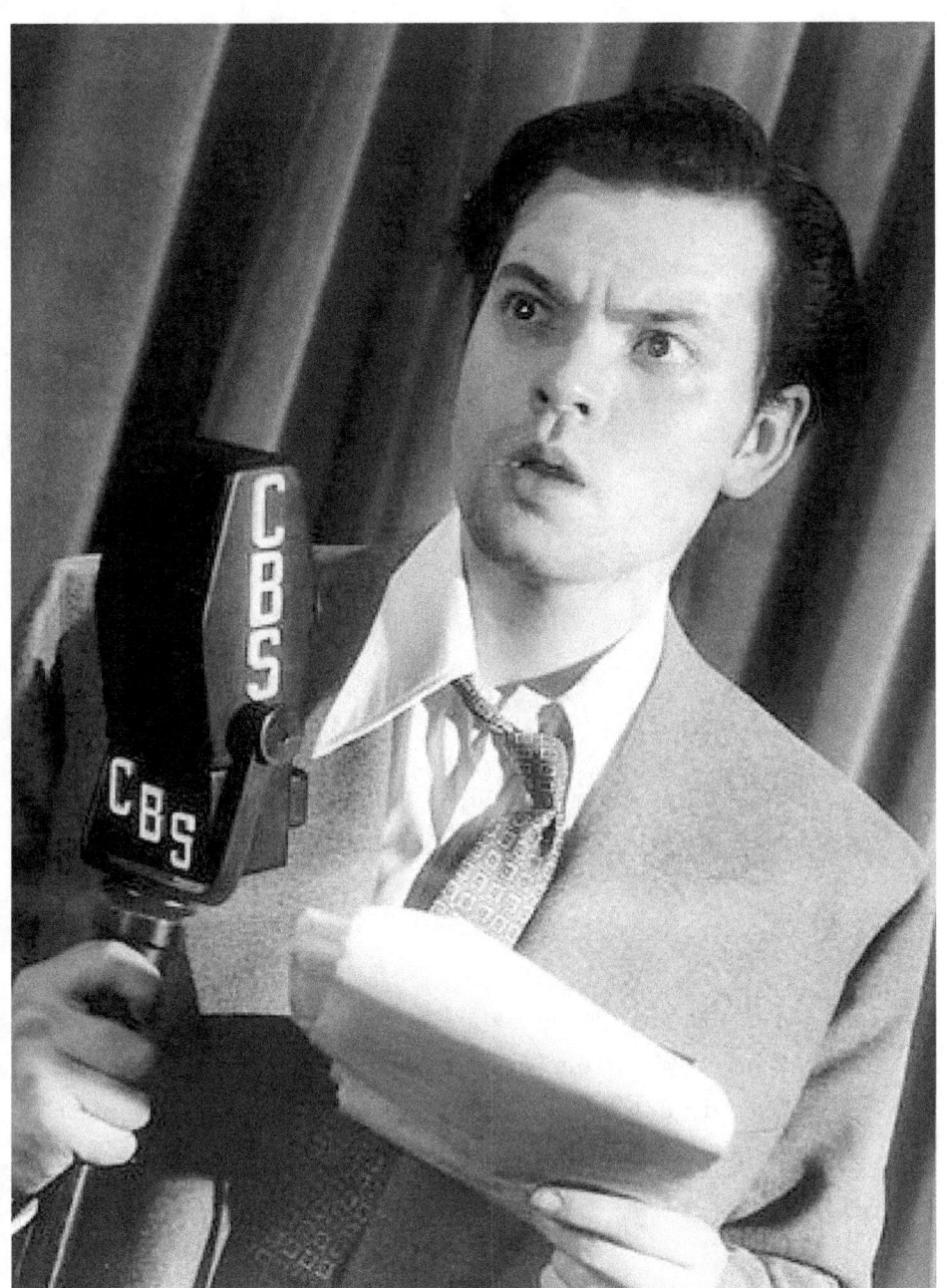

The Nation's No. 1 bogey man, back in 1938.

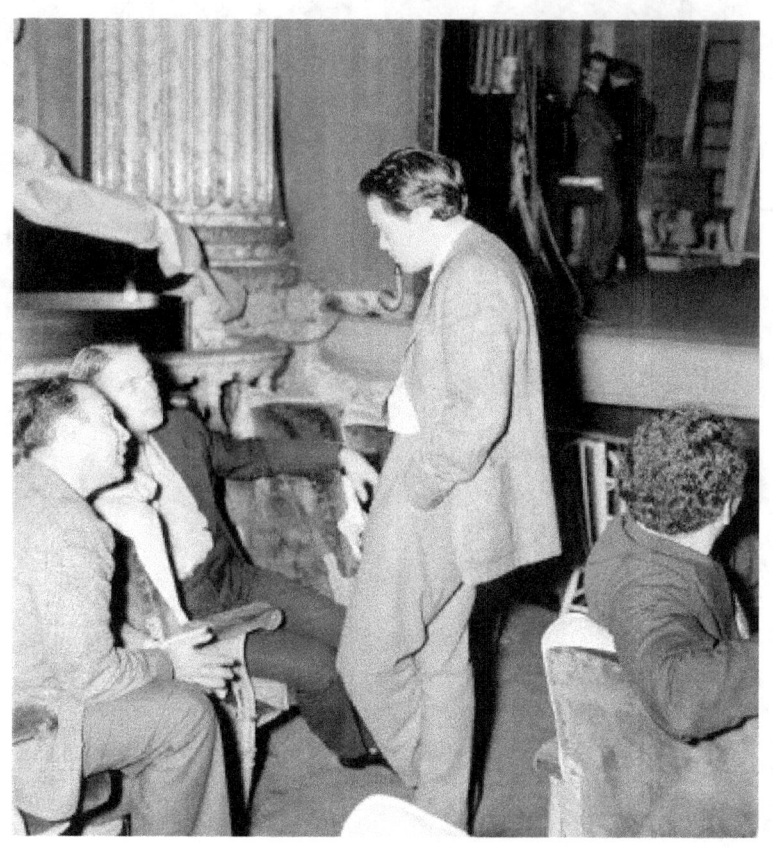

Welles during a 1936 theatre rehearsal.

It was in 1938 that Welles and the Mercury Theatre On Air put on their notorious War of the Worlds production, fooling large amounts of the country into believing a Martian attack was actually under way. "I think we underrated the prestige of radio at that moment, anything that was said on the radio was automatically true," Welles recalled. "After that nobody ever believed anything on the radio and, Pearl Harbour, the day of Pearl Harbour in America I was doing a radio broadcast which was interrupted with the announcement that Pearl Harbour had been attacked and of course everybody in America said it's rather bad taste to do it again."

Welles became famous on an even wider level, attracting the attention of Hollywood, who began to seek him out as early as 1938. It wasn't until August of 1939 that he eventually signed a film deal with RKO, insistent of course that he be allowed final cut and full control of the movie he would be making. (One needs to add the film segments Welles shot for his stage production, Too Much Johnson, as his debut directorial work, though it was never released at the time and has only since been restored and put into an order resembling a film.)

So it was RKO Pictures who managed to sway him, for studio boss George J. Schafer saw Welles as a star in every way. It's easy to see why Welles was tempted by the RKO contract, adding to the final cut the fact he was to star in, direct and write the picture he would be taking on. How much Hollywood was willing to bend for Welles really illustrates how much faith they had in his work. That Kane was such a masterpiece though, makes you wonder why no film studio ever gave him such freedom again. Surely, you would think, that the system might twig on that maybe Welles knew something they didn't. "I could make a better picture than Kane," Welles said in 1960, "but no one has ever given me a second chance."

The whole idea had generated from a thematic experiment Orson had in mind. Though he is remembered solely as the film's creator, it was a collaborative effort with screenwriter Herman J. Mankiewicz that resulted in the Kane we know and love.

"I'd been nursing an old notion," Welles told Peter Bogdanovich, "the idea of telling the same thing several times – and showing exactly the same scene from wholly different points of view. Basically, the idea Rashomon used later on. Mank liked it, so we started searching for the man it was going to be about. Some big American figure – couldn't be a politician, because you'd have to pinpoint him. Howard Hughes was the first idea. But we got pretty quickly to the press lords. The actual writing came only after lots of talk, naturally, just the two of us, yelling at each other – not too angrily. It withered away from what was originally intended. I wanted the man to seem a very different person depending on who was talking about him. 'Rosebud' was Mank's, and the many-sided gimmick was mine. Rosebud remained, because it was the only way we could find to get off, as they used to say in vaudeville. It manages to work, but I'm still not too keen about it, and I don't think that he was, either. The whole shtick is the sort of thing that can finally date, in some funny way."

In the hands of anyone else, Kane could still have been a decent mystery picture, a genuinely affecting story delivering a painful punch at its end. But Orson gives it a scale, gravitas and grace which instantly elevated it above any other film of the time. Watching it in the context and thematic confines of its era, Kane stands out as something that is quite simply on another level; the brave experimentation, the free cameras, the reinvention of the rules of conventional filmmaking. One still sees and feels its influence today, despite Welles' genius techniques now being so easy to duplicate with CGI and high tech gear.

What makes Kane so extraordinary in its directorial style is the fact that Welles was a newcomer. Yes he had filmed backdrop segments for his play Too Much Johnson, and also goofed around doing arty silent experiments with his friends years earlier, but this was uncharted territory for him. That the studio let him in the director's chair at all is truly remarkable. The fact it wouldn't happen today tells us that there is probably a film genius out there not being given his chance to shine.

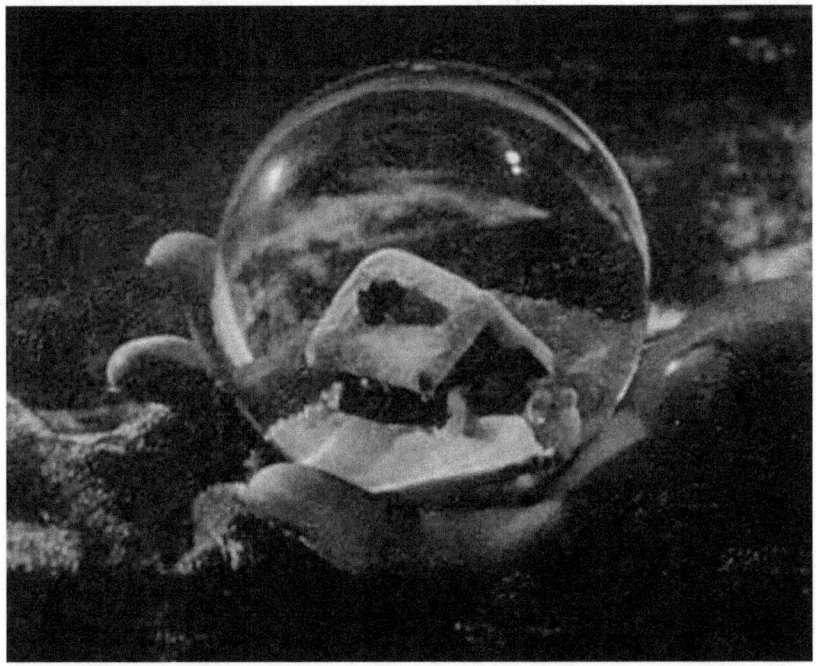

"When I made Kane, I didn't know enough about movies, and I was constantly encouraged by [cinematographer Gregg] Toland, who said, under the influence of Ford, 'Carry everything in one shot – don't do anything else.' In other words, play scenes through without cutting, and don't shoot any alternate version. That was Toland in my ear. And secondly, I didn't know how to have all kinds of choices. All I could think of to do was what was going to be on the screen in the final version. Also, I had a wonderful cast..."

Orson kept the film's mystery alive by never really explaining every facet of the film. As he said, "I don't think a moviemaker should explain what he means. About anything. Leave it to the customers. Why spoil things for people who enjoy finding their own meanings?" Such an attitude to his own work only mythologised it even more.

While Orson hated it and said even by 1960 that it hadn't held up, Rosebud is the thing which has endured most of all in Kane, ensuring its part in pop culture for all eternity. But Kane the man, the myth and the legend remains the focal point. It begins with a scene from his death bed, dropping the snow globe which shatters beautifully before the camera, in utter silence. We then enter into the life of Kane himself, a rich newspaper publisher, and the journey journalist Jerry Thompson makes in discovering the true meaning of Kane's final word... Rosebud. Getting to the bottom of the Kane mystery, Thompson presents us with a vivid portrait of the man, and never personally unravels the enigma. However, we the viewer *do* get to the bottom of it, the camera revealing the true meaning of Rosebud, the innocence Kane was perhaps hanging on to, despite all the things that happened to him. The idea that an old man on his death bed might think back, hazily, to a treasured childhood artefact, which is then seen as junk and burnt to dust, is a heartbreaking notion. How many of us, in our final moments, our minds half elsewhere to a land beyond this world, might drift off back to an image, an item, a memory, from deep in our past?

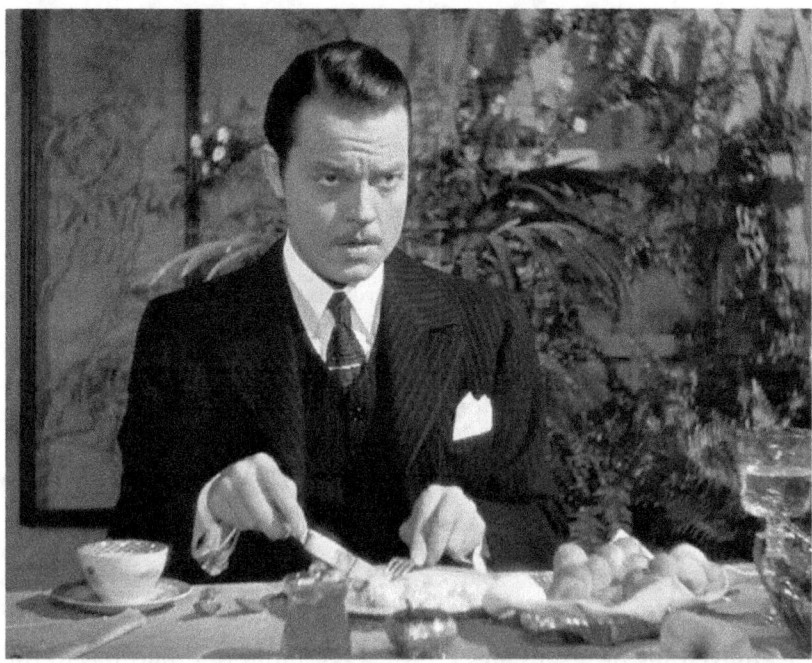

Interviewing Orson, Peter Bogdanovich asked Orson if he had a personal Rosebud, a part of his past he wanted to go back to. He had once said Woodstock Illinois was that place, but to his filmmaking friend, he opened up more. "No... I have no wish to be back there... Just one part of it, maybe. One place. My father lived sometimes in China, and partly in a tiny country hotel he'd bought in a village called Grand Detour, Illinois. It had a population of 130. Formerly it was ten thousand, but then the railroad didn't go through. And there was this hotel which had been built to service the covered wagons on their way west through southern Illinois. My father spent a few months of his year there, entertaining a few friends. Our servants were all retired or 'resting' from show business. A gentleman called Rattlesnake-Oil Emery was handyman. One of the waitresses had done bird calls in a tent show. My father was very fond of people like that. Well, where I do see some kind of Rosebud, perhaps, is in that world of Grand Detour."

For Orson, this could have been decades earlier. "A childhood there was like a childhood back in the 1870s. No electric light, horse-drawn buggies, a completely anachronistic, old-fashioned, early-Tarkington, rural kind of life, with a country store that had above it a ballroom with an old dance floor with springs in it, so that folks would feel light on their feet. When I was little, nobody had danced up there for many years, but I used to sneak up at night and dance by moonlight with the dust rising from the floor... Grand Detour was one of those lost worlds, one of those Edens that you get thrown out of. It really was kind of invented by my father. He's the one who kept out the cars and the electric lights. It was one of the 'Merrie Englands.' Imagine: he smoked his own sausages. You'd wake up in the morning to the sound of the folks in the bake house, and the smells... I feel as though I've had a childhood in the last century from those short summers."

Asked if he had a fondness for the past, Orson simply replied, "Oh yes. For that Eden people lose... It's a theme that interests me. A nostalgia for the garden – it's a recurring theme in all our civilization."

For all the nonsense spouted by Orson doubters that he really was not the man behind Kane (Pauline Kael's ludicrous anti Orson article on the film is an abomination), it is clear from Orson's later directorial work, and even the segments we have seen from his abandoned and unfinished movies, that the visual inventiveness, iconic imagery and immortal moments are down to Orson being behind the camera. One must only look at a scene from The Magnificent Ambersons, the dizzying party in The Other Side of the Wind, or the sheer gorgeousness of Touch Of Evil to see that Kane is Orson through and through. In not knowing the rules, Orson was able to instinctively set new ones, and had Kane been made by an established Hollywood director, there could have been elements of cliché and predictability, phoney set ups and back drops. Alas, Orson ensures every scene, every moment, every background and prop is a work of pure artistry. Even now, there are very few, if any, films which can match it for its look alone.

The age old argument of Kane not being or indeed *being* the best picture of all time is a debate that no one will ever really get to the bottom of. It's all subjective, though on a technical level you could argue that it achieved what would have seemed to be impossible at the time. The way Orson brings us *inside* the story, *within* the events unfolding, rather than showing them to us on a flat canvas (as was the Hollywood way of the time) should not be forgotten. If we are talking on a level of influence and innovation, Kane is undoubtedly at the top of the list. Though others have come since, no film has influenced the director, the maverick and the auteur like Kane. Ken Russell, Stanley Kubrick, Steven Spielberg, Terry Gilliam - these are just a few names from a long list of filmmakers who owe much of their lives to Welles' cinematic discoveries. If it's even Orson Welles' finest film is another consideration to be pondered, but either way it's remarkable filmmaking of the sort we will never see again, and definitely not released within the Hollywood machine.

Of course, the fact that Orson had Gregg Toland as his cameraman, the leading one at the time, meant that he would have the right help by his side. But as Toland noted to Orson, the fact that he was left to his own devices as much as possible would mean that this film would look different to all the others. "I am tired of working with people who know too much about it," Toland had said. Orson also recalled that Toland told him that everything to learn about film could be taught in three hours... if you are good enough and have the talent of course. Welles admitted that if he himself had come out with those words, it would have been a case of pomposity. However, coming from Toland, one can only wonder. (An added note: Orson came out with something similar once at a Q and A with some film students, telling them they should quit school and get outside, for they could learn everything they needed within three hours.)

Technical wizardry aside, at the centre of this film is one of the finest performances in the history of film. Though he had provided voice over for two films previous to this (Ernest Hemingway's The Spanish Earth and Edward Ludwig's Swiss Family Robinson, 1937 and 1940), this is his official on screen acting debut. It's an effort so staggering and towering, intimidating in fact, that it seems a shame it is so often over shadowed by the film which somehow manages to contain it.

As Kane, Welles spans the ages, from his 20s to his 70s, in each guise as convincing as the last. Young and vital, he is the epitome of youthful ambition; as old man, he has the kind of aged beaten quality the real life Orson never had. But this is a staggering feat, and regardless of what costume or disguise he wears throughout, it's all in the eyes. When Orson said it took him so much concentration to muster up the kind of acting and emotion someone like Gary Cooper could do naturally, then it was worth the effort. Orson can say more in a glance, or a mere movement of the eyes, than most actors can with a paragraph of the world's best dialogue. It's in the human connection where Orson reaches you, using masks, aids, beards and wigs as a mere tool, not a crutch to get to the core of the performance. Writer, director and actor, Welles packed a triple whammy, and it's hard to think of anyone matching his work in Kane in all these three areas. The reason it works so well is because it meant so much to the man, and that he managed to keep full control of the picture as it came to fruition.

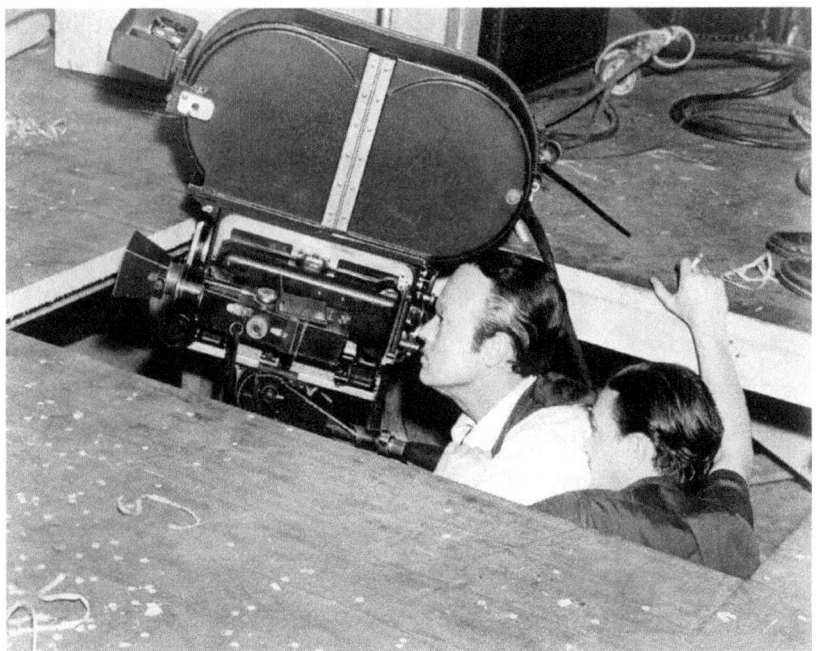

At the time, Citizen Kane only did respectable business, still managing to make back its budget twice over; but it was in the reviews that it excelled and was immediately elevated above all the other films being made in Hollywood, and the whole world for that matter. "Citizen Kane is a triumph for Orson Welles," Variety wrote at the time, "who overnight, so to speak, joins the top ranks of box office film personalities."

The New York Times' ecstatic review kind of summed up the reaction to the movie, when they wrote: "Within the withering spotlight as no other film has ever been before, Orson Welles's Citizen Kane had is world première at the Palace last evening. And now that the wraps are off, the mystery has been exposed and Mr. Welles and the RKO directors have taken the much-debated leap, it can be safely stated that suppression of this film would have been a crime. For, in spite of some disconcerting lapses and strange ambiguities in the creation of the principal character, Citizen Kane is far and away the most surprising and cinematically exciting motion picture to be seen here in many a moon. As a matter of fact, it comes close to being the most sensational film ever made in Hollywood."

Though Welles often pointed out there was just as much backlash as there was acclaim, it is the rave reviews where one cannot help but be drawn to. Did this success go to his head? Welles thinks not, even though he was aware of how new this all was.

"It was perfectly natural for an actor to direct himself," Orson told the BBC, revealing the pitfalls of being the auteur through and through, "but no one had done it since von Stroheim. It was unheard of. And then that I should be the author and absolute producer. Of course the producers hated me the most, because if I could do all those things, then what is the need for a producer?"

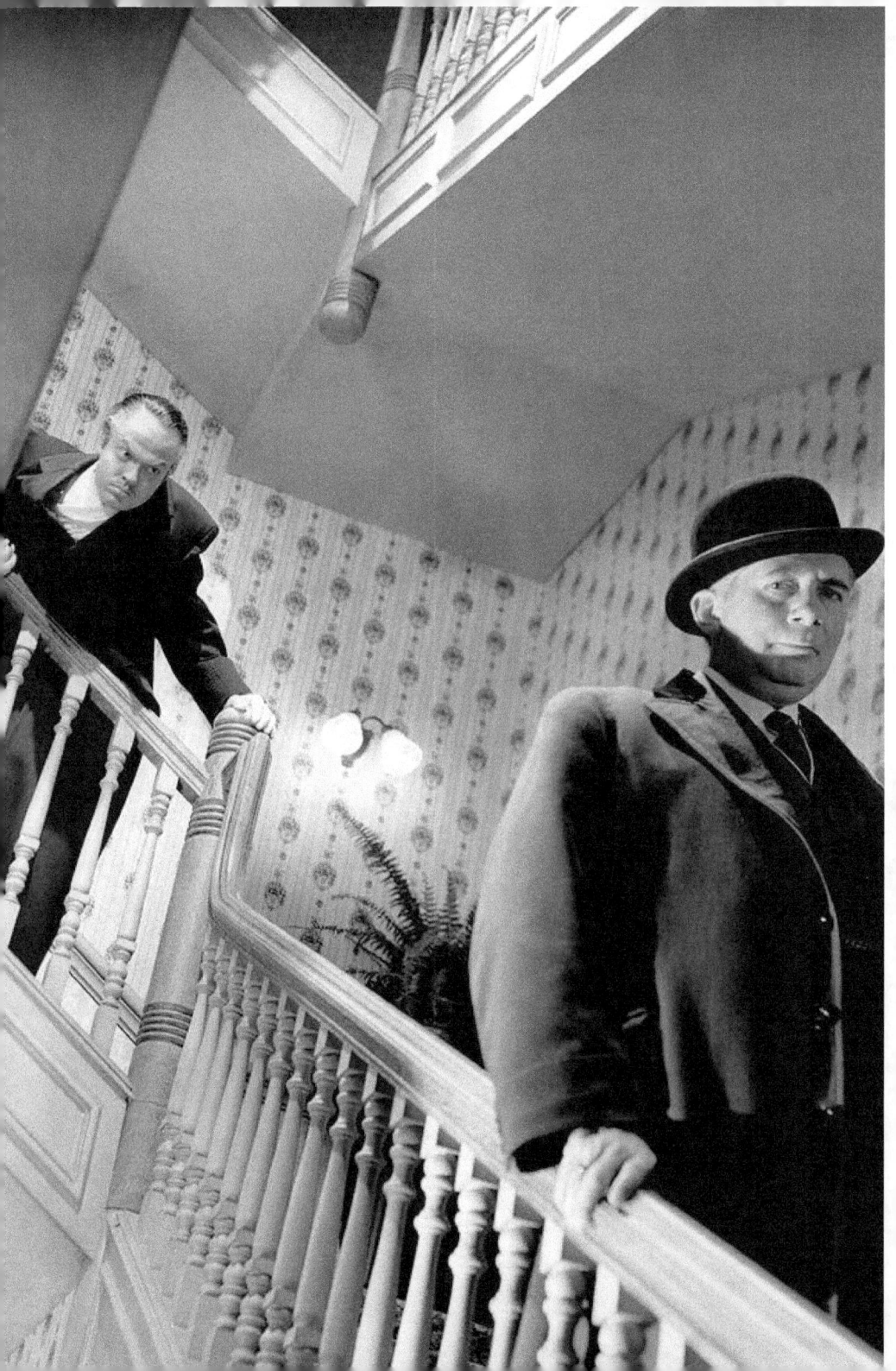

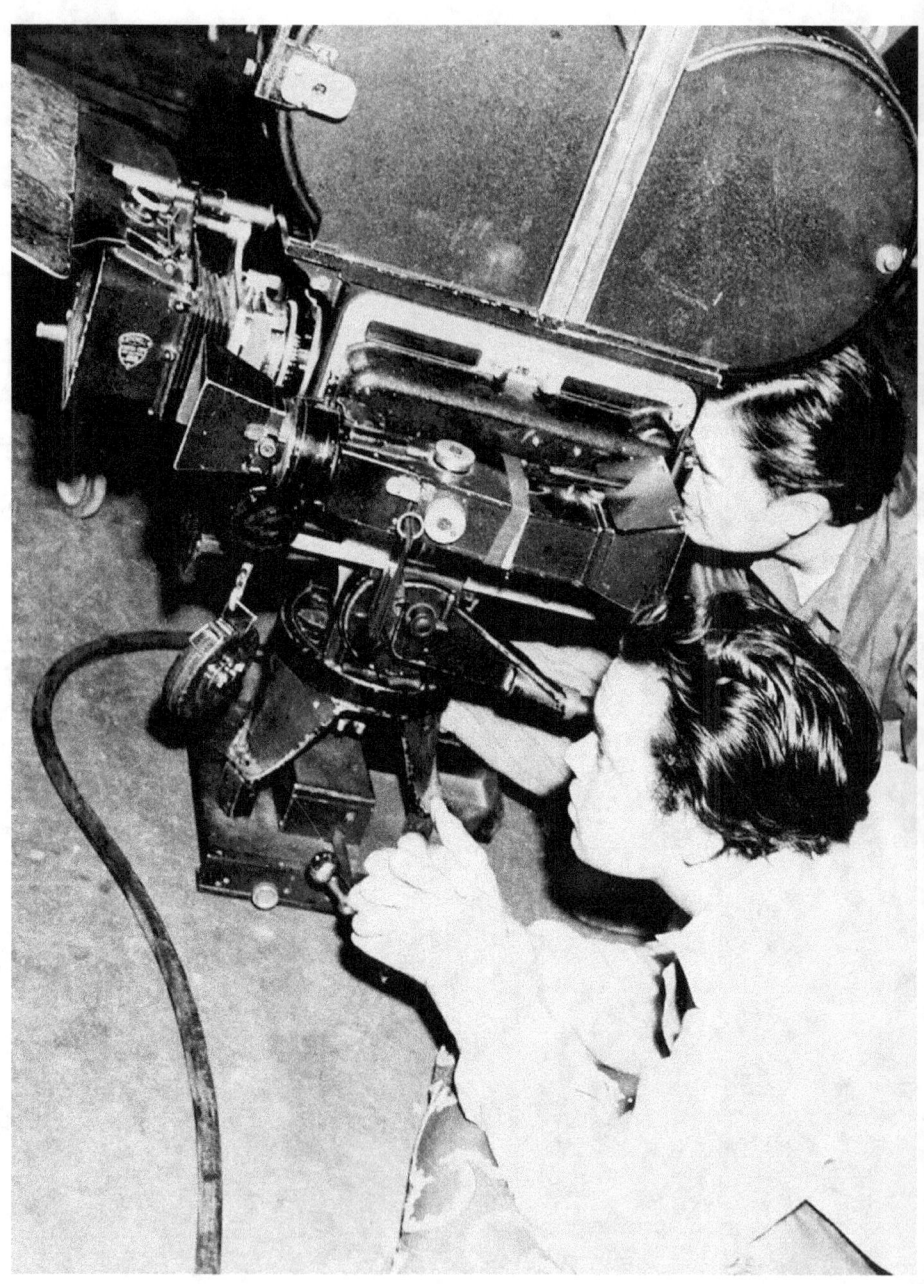

Welles and Toland direct Citizen Kane

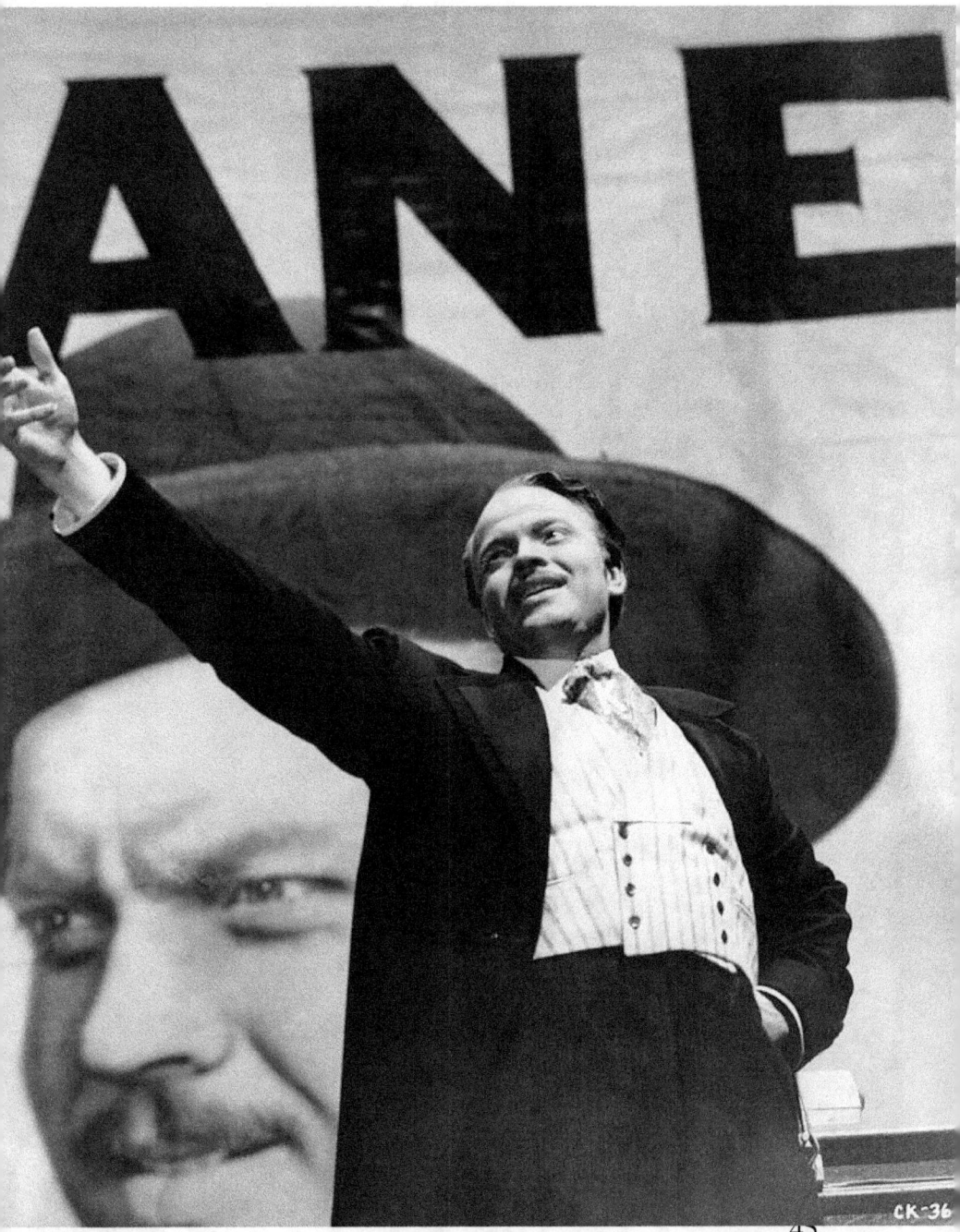

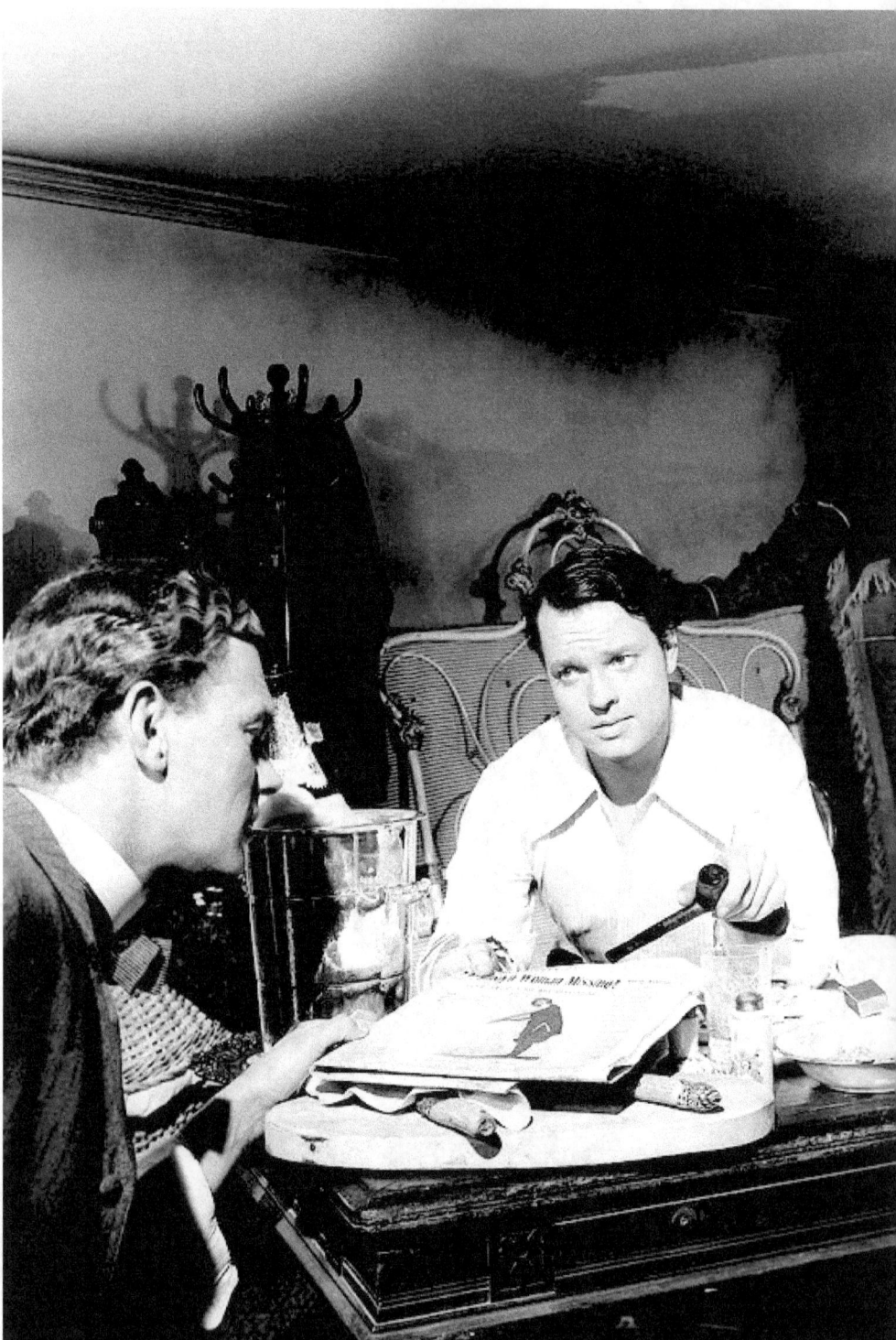

If everyone could do what Orson did - produce, direct, star, write, design, conceive - then there would be thousands of films as effective, powerful and moving as Citizen Kane. But of course there was only one Orson, and there is only one Citizen Kane. Whether he ever lived up to it again or not is a matter of opinion (personally I think he did, particularly with Chimes of Midnight and now the Other Side of the Wind), but the film is certainly a one off, an important moment in time for filmmakers, artists and anyone interested in cinema to be inspired by again and again for centuries.

A Cinematic Tragedy

In The American Dreamer, Laurence Schiller's documentary about the making of Dennis Hopper's 1971 lost masterpiece The Last Movie, the bearded, bedraggled Hopper becomes frustrated with the interference of the film studio into his great masterpiece. From his mouth comes the immortal utterance - "Now I know how Orson Welles felt when he made The Magnificent Ambersons." It's the ultimate statement of artistic violation, the pain of having one's art torn to shreds by the careless executives. In Hopper's case, they just wanted to know what he was spending their money on; in Orson Welles' case, they butchered a classic, and expected him to stand back and just watch it all happen.

The story of the Ambersons, the richest family in America as conceived by Booth Tarkington in his Pulitzer Prize winner, had long been of interest to Welles. Only three years before making the film, Orson had arranged the radio version of the story with the Mercury Players, playing the character of George. But why was he so interested in the book? He must undoubtedly have seen similarities between the Ambersons and his own family, a wealthy one from the Mid West with ties to the automobile trade. Perhaps it was this that ensured the film and story meant so much to Orson, which of course made the fact the studios overthrew him even more tragic.

Ambersons remained a film which was painful for Welles to think about. There's a story that concerns Welles finally sitting down to watch his slashed masterpiece in 1980, with his good friend and confidant Henry Jaglom. After the first hour, Orson switched off the TV, declaring, "from here on, it becomes their picture." Their idea of a good picture was something much safer than what Orson had in mind, and RKO took to the task of mutilating his vision. Seeing as a screening of Welles' vision of the movie had gone wrong, the studio opted to release the Robert Wise edit, betraying the maverick. Clearly, Kane had been a one off, a one time only deal from a system which massaged his ego just to get him roped in. From here on in, it would never be as easy again. Ambersons drew a line in the sand.

Yet the film did OK and received many plaudits, and is still remembered fondly by Orson admirers all over the world. A film of one family disintegrating both class wise and financially, it looked to be the ideal follow up to his monstrous Kane, and indeed could have been so. As a metaphor for the advancements of technology, the need for progress and the urge to cease such action, it was vintage Welles fare. After all, this was the man who enjoyed a childhood without automobiles and 20th century normalities, and longed for that age in the back of his mind.

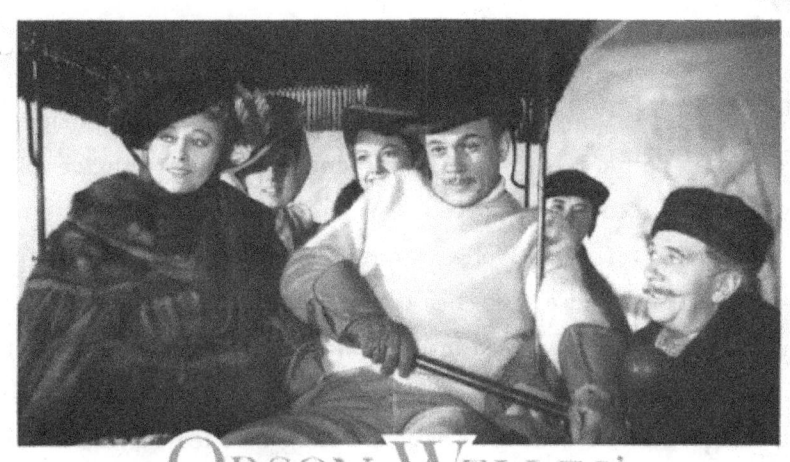

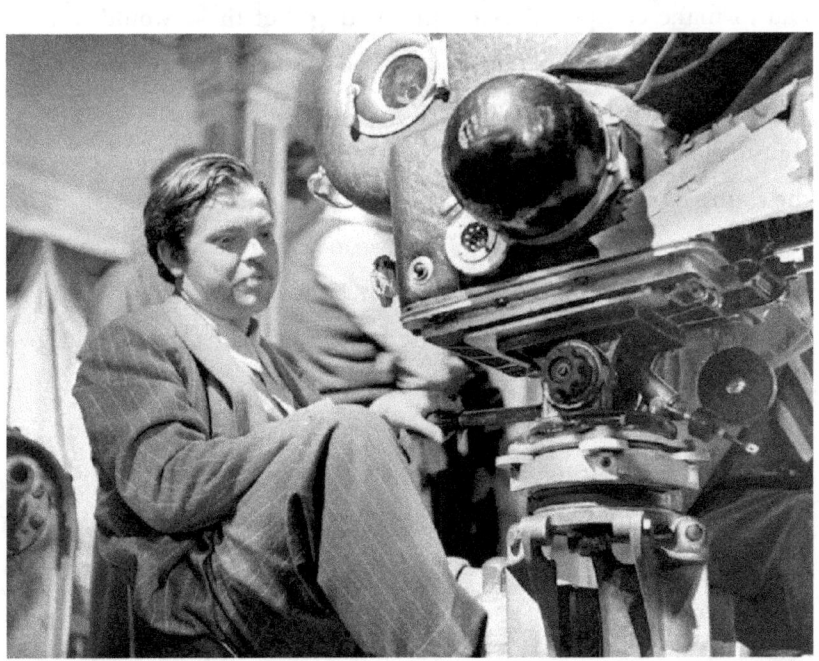

Unfortunately, Toland, his Kane cinematographer, could not be hired, so Orson got Stanley Cortez on board instead. He did however manage to employ the services of the legendary film music composer Bernard Herrmann, the man who had brought genuine gleeful life to the speedy pace of Kane. The talent was there, so was the script. So where did Welles go wrong? Well firstly, he failed to get the final cut clause into his contract, meaning RKO could do whatever they pleased with his film. It didn't help that Welles went off to Brazil to make a documentary straight after the shoot, as part of the government's Good Neighbor Policy, thus leaving his film to the mercies of the studio. In Orson's defence though, even if he had stuck around, there wasn't much he could have done, considering the studio's control over his picture. "Even if I'd stayed in the US to finish The Magnificent Ambersons," he later remarked, "I would've had to make compromises on the editing, but these would've been mine and not the fruit of confused and often semi-hysterical committees. If I had been there myself, I would have found my own solutions and saved the picture in a form which would have carried the stamp of my own effort."

As a film, Ambersons is so often overlooked in favour of Kane, and if it is discussed, it often seems to be the "maverick" element, the fight of the little filmmaker against the huge monstrous studio that gets the air time. It's the very idea of this romanticised vision which grabs the interest, and indeed it is a tempting cliché to fall for. But one must remember this was not a well worn cliché before the butchering of the Ambersons movie debacle. This was the first time an auteur, especially one on the scale of Welles' acclaim, had been so cruelly treated by the studio, even after delivering a solid gold masterpiece. Everyone from Terry Gilliam to Ken Russell knows what it is to fight for a good budget, for artistic control and, if he is very lucky, the final cut. But Orson was the first of the mavericks, the prime filmmaker taking on the machine. He was to be the guinea pig. In this case he lost, but at least a decent film was still retrieved from the whole manic drama.

The sad part of all this, is the fact that Welles had so much faith in the work, even if it did have a darker edge to it than what most movie goers were used to. "Of course I expected that there would be an uproar about a picture which, by any ordinary American standards, was much darker than anybody was making pictures," Welles later said. "There was just a built-in dread of the downbeat movie, and I knew I'd have that to face, but I thought I had a movie so good—I was absolutely certain of its value, much more than of Kane... It's a tremendous preparation for the boarding house... and the terrible walk of George Minafer when he gets his comeuppance. And without that, there wasn't any plot. It's all about some rich people fighting in their house."

But Orson knew he was torn. He could not leave Brazil, for he was in effect serving his country, making his film It's All True. Unfit for service during World War 2, he was officially Roosevelt's Goodwill Ambassador for South America. However, had he been given final cut, he never would have gone there.

"But I couldn't walk out on a job which had diplomatic overtones," Orson said, knowing full well he was stuck. "I was representing America in Brazil, you see. I was a prisoner of the Good Neighbor Policy. That's what made it such a nightmare. I couldn't walk out on Mr. Roosevelt's Good Neighbor Policy with the biggest single thing that they'd done on the cultural level, and simply walk away. And I couldn't get my film in my hands."

For Orson, the worst part of all was the fact the studio changed what he saw as the pivotal scene, giving the film a happy ending which ruined the poeticism completely. When Orson suggested they keep his downbeat ending and go out on a jolly sounding credits sequence, they sternly turned him down. Still, you can't blame a guy for trying!

Over thirty years later, Orson revealed to Peter Bogdanovich that he had planned to race back in and re shoot the end of the film with the cast members who were still alive. Nothing came to fruition, but one can ponder on just what the results might have been had Orson pulled it off.

"Yes, I had an outside chance to finish it again just a couple of years ago," he said in the early 70s, "but I couldn't swing it. The fellow who was going to buy the film for me disappeared from view. The idea was to take the actors who are still alive now — Cotten, Baxter, Moorehead, Holt — and do quite a new end to the movie, twenty years after. Maybe that way we could have got a new release and a large audience to see it for the first time. You see, the basic intention was to portray a golden world—almost one of memory—and then show what it turns into. Having set up this dream town of the "good old days," the whole point was to show the automobile wrecking it— not only the family but the town. All this is out. What's left is only the first six reels. Then there's a kind of arbitrary bringing back down the curtain by a series of clumsy, quick devices. The bad, black world was supposed to be too much for people. My whole third act is lost because of all the hysterical tinkering that went on. And it *was* hysterical. Everybody they could find was cutting it."

Still, the reviews for Ambersons say it all, and the picture itself received four Oscar nominations. The New York Times were almost as ecstatic as they had been for Kane only one year earlier (yes, Orson really did make these two classics right after one another), writing "With only two pictures to his credit, last year's extraordinary Citizen Kane and now Booth Tarkington's The Magnificent Ambersons, Orson Welles has demonstrated beyond doubt that the screen is his medium. He has an eloquent, if at times grandiose, flair for the dramatic which only the camera can fully capture and he has a truly wondrous knack for making his actors, even the passing bit player, behave like genuine human beings. And yet, with all his remarkable talent, Mr. Welles still apparently refuses to make concessions to popular appeal. The Capitol's new film, however magnificently executed, is a relentlessly sombre drama on a barren theme. All in all, The Magnificent Ambersons is an exceptionally well-made film, dealing with a subject scarcely worth the attention which has been lavished upon it."

As great as the movie is, even in its savaged form, it's infinitely more notable as a symbol of a changing time, the point when Orson lost his heart and soul when it came to believing in what Hollywood had to offer him. It was soul crushing, and Orson was never the same again. He went on to direct films that were just as strong, better even, but he was a casualty, a necessary one, from whom every filmmaker who followed in his wake would learn a valuable lesson. Few directors have balanced artistic and commercial success, and possibly only Stanley Kubrick ever got close to the sheer artistry Welles achieved in these films; but importantly he managed to keep his control, the rights to the final cut, with integrity intact. Welles would have killed for such luxuries...

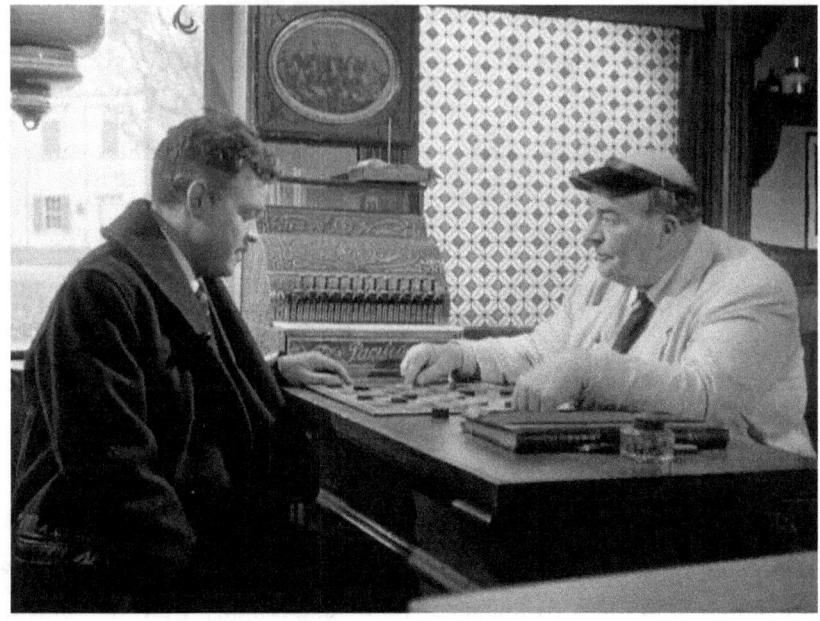

"Not Glow in the Dark..."

Since Orson had donated his many talents solely to the movies, the artistic form he so loved but found a challenge due to the rules of the industry, he had experienced highs and lows. The high was, of course, his masterpiece, the miraculously excellent Citizen Kane. The low had been The Magnificent Ambersons, a passion project that had suffered the harshest blows of the film business. There was also an in between; for instance, Orson was marvellous in Robert Stevenson's 1943 Jane Eyre. As a filmmaker though, not merely a screen actor, Welles was fighting battles.

After the disappointment of his abandoned third RKO film, It's All True, which the company reportedly dumped in the sea rather than attempting to salvage anything from, Welles went on to star alongside Dolores del Rio and Joseph Cotton in Journey Into Fear, an adaptation of the spy novel by Eric Ambler. He was in fact originally down as the official director, but work on the Ambersons meant that he could not officially fill the role, even though he did direct some scenes. Instead, Norman Foster took over direction, and in the end Welles and his Mercury acting friends were fired by RKO. Again, Welles was pushed out of the edit, the film being left to Mark Robson.

Still, in this case, everything turned out OK. Everyone involved does a good job in bringing the film to life (though it was not so well received at the time), and Welles is fantastic as Col. Haki. Seeing him put in a briefer acting turn and still managing to steal the picture from all concerned, highlights his sheer charisma and talent, even only a couple of picture into his screen career. Some cite it as a proper Welles film, and I must say I find it fits neatly into the line of his early directorial efforts. Others however, view it somewhere off to the right, an RKO contractual filler which he didn't really have all that much interest in. Either way, it's a strong film and any Welles fan will get a kick from his performance.

Reviews were rather muted, especially when compared to his first two directorial works. Variety, who had been so excited by Kane, murmured "In Journey into Fear, Orson Welles' third release for RKO, he handles only the production reins and takes one of the character leads but leaves direction in the hands of Norman Foster. Picture attempts to catch attention through series of dramatic peaks, but misses that mark by a considerable margin, being too stagey and talky. Joseph Cotten is the pivotal character – an American naval ordnance engineer returning to the US from Istanbul. Welles delivers an above-par characterization as the Turkish secret police chief. Cotten is okay in the lead, despite the fact the writers present him as a rather weakling hero throughout. Direction by Foster is deliberate and slow, pausing too much on unimportant incidentals. Adaptation of Eric Ambler's novel was prepared by Welles and Cotten, and there's nothing new in technique or treatment."

"Out of Eric Ambler's thriller, Journey Into Fear, Orson Welles and his perennial Mercury Company have made an uneven but generally imaginative and exciting tale of terror," wrote the New York Times. "Less ambitious than any of the company's previous productions, the new film at the Palace is nevertheless many notches above the garden variety regularly sent to Broadway. To select outstanding performances would be to name practically the entire cast—in which Mr. Welles's characterization of the Turkish police chief is the only one which is overdrawn. Joseph Cotten gives a deftly suggestive performance as the pursued expert; Agnes Moorehead adds another exacerbating portrait of a shrewish woman, and Jack Moss—also Welles's business manager—nearly steals every scene in which he appears as the pudgy-faced killer. Despite its lapses, Journey Into Fear is still a terse invitation to heart failure by fright."

While it would have been impossible for Welles to keep the press happy picture after picture, the reception of Journey Into Fear was undoubtedly disappointing and grimly muffled, especially considering the dizzying acclaim thrust upon Kane. Perhaps though, deep down, Welles was a little relieved the film wasn't met with such wild hysteria. Huge success had never been his true aim; it was experimentation and creativity which appealed to him. Now, just maybe, he could get back on with his work again.

The boy wonder was a boy no more, and by the mid 40s had reached the grand age of... well, only thirty. Three decades into his life and he had achieved so much already. After a misfire or two on the big screen, Orson took on the direction (and indeed the uncredited writing, alongside Anthony Veiller and Decla Dunning) for 1946's The Stranger, often wrongly viewed as a routine thriller for which he took the money and ran. It is also among Orson's least favourite of his own films, which is odd, as I feel it's a very effective and strong picture, visually extremely strong and full of top notch performances.

The film is about a war crime investigations man, played by Edward G Robinson, who is hunting down a fugitive Nazi, played marvellously by Welles himself. Filmed at the back end of 1945, it was originally intended as a directorial vehicle for John Huston, who producer Sam Spiegel had in mind from the start. When Huston became unavailable, Welles was approached. Signing a stiff contract where he promised not to challenge the creativity and direction of the picture - basically be the director and nothing else - Orson was forced to zip his mouth shut and get on with the picture. Considering his obvious discomfort with such constraints, it's surprising that the resulting picture is as rich and enjoyable as it is. Though he claimed nothing in the film was really his, there is a Wellesian atmosphere throughout, and clearly Orson put a lot of his talent, energy and individuality into this moody noir tale. It feels like a Welles film, even if the man himself claims it not to be.

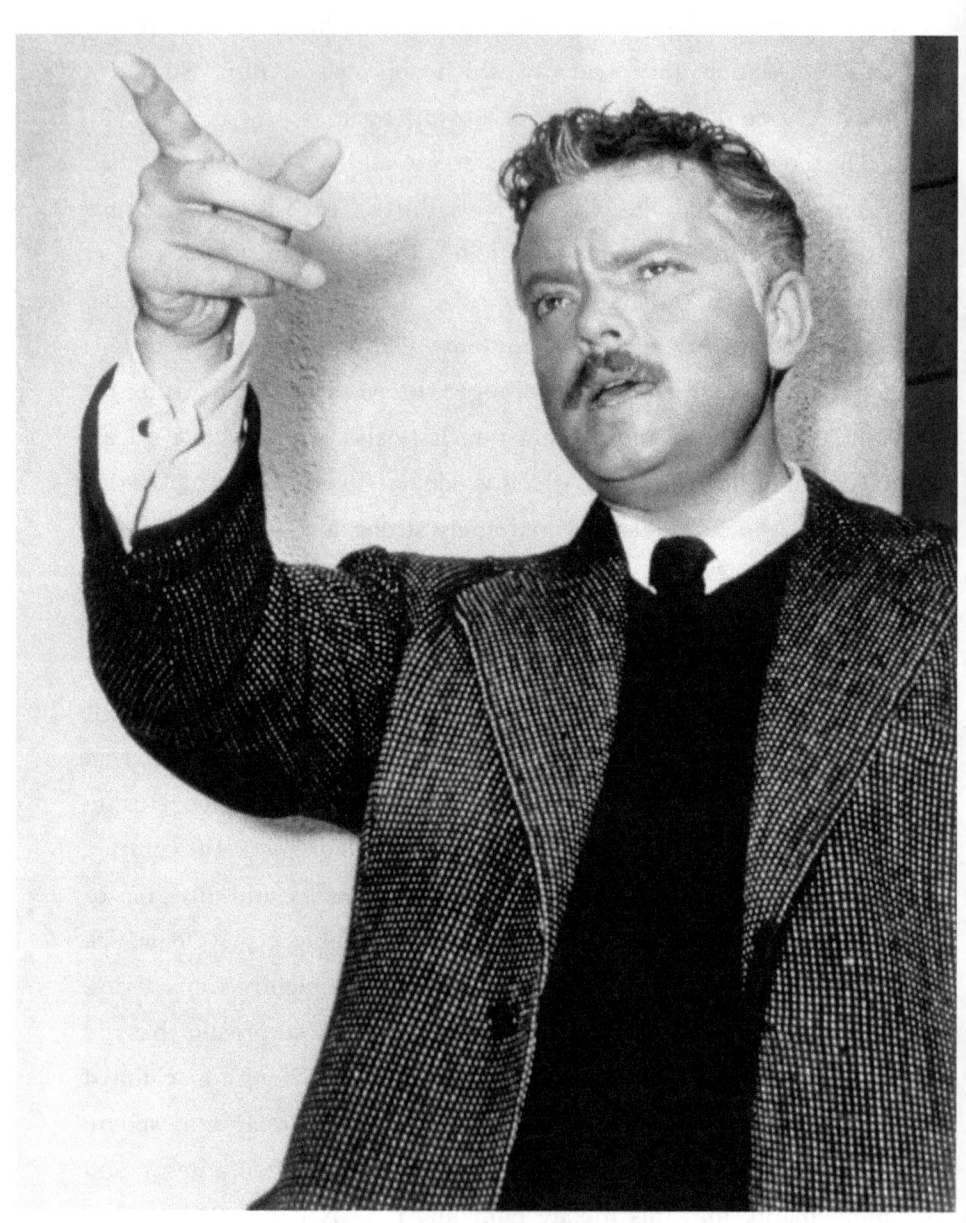

Orson directs The Stranger

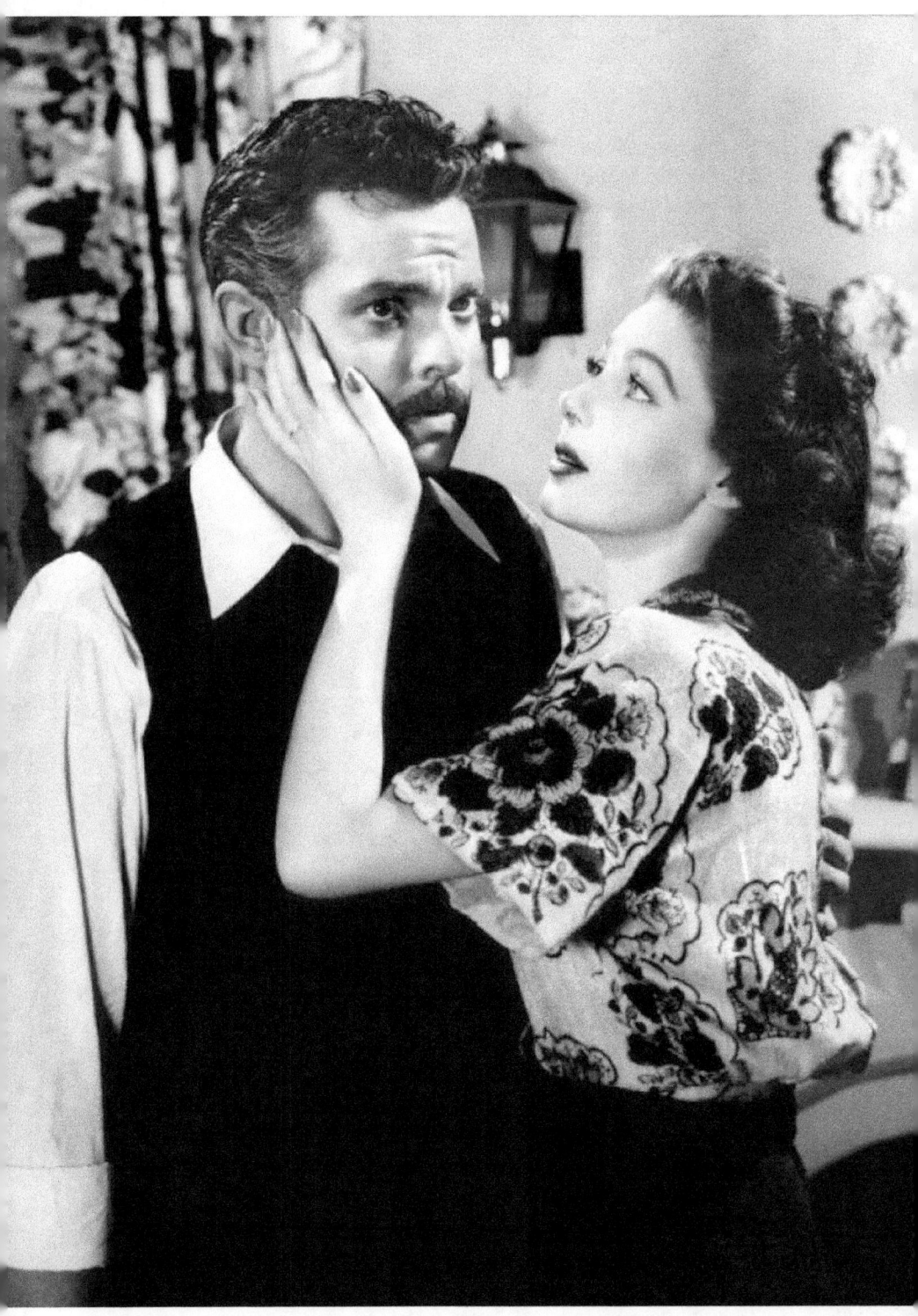

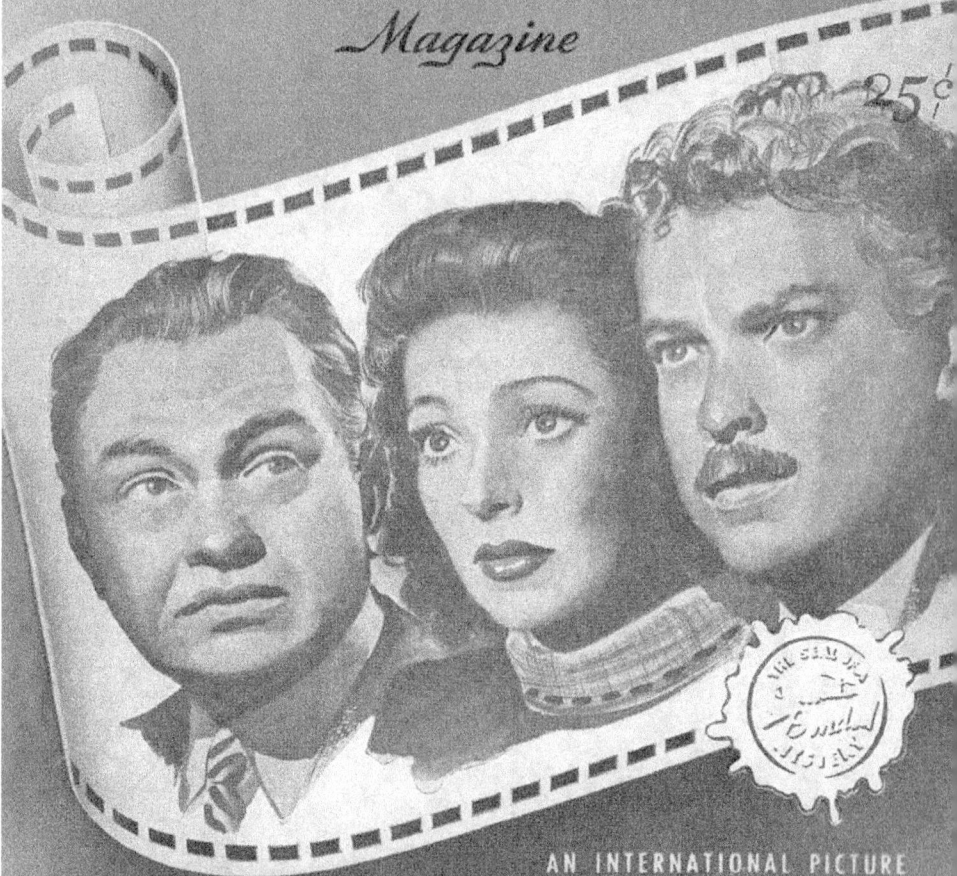

JULY — AUGUST

MOVIE ★ MYSTERY

Magazine

25¢

AN INTERNATIONAL PICTURE
STARRING

EDWARD G. ROBINSON • LORETTA YOUNG • ORSON WELLES
IN "THE STRANGER"

Complete Novelization in this Issue . . . PLUS 9 SPECIAL FEATURES

Recalling working with Robinson, the legendary man himself, Welles had an interesting story to tell. "I didn't know him at all. And he had gone into a big sulk the first week. I couldn't understand what it was about and he said, You keep shooting me on my bad side. Now can you imagine Eddie Robinson having a bad side? And I was shooting him that way because Loretta Young's side was the other one, you see. So I told her about it and she said, All right, shoot me on my bad side and keep him happy. But he was an immensely effective actor. And he was very good in the picture."

Welles was rather telling years later when explaining his decision to direct The Stranger. He says he did it "to show people that I didn't glow in the dark, you know. That I could say 'action' and 'cut' just like all the other fellas." Orson did indeed know how to perform the basics of filmmaking, but he also lifted this potentially tired idea into another realm all together, an "almost perfect, near classic" as people have often referred to it. It should also be mentioned how magnificent Welles' performance actually is here, moustached, suited and utterly mysterious.

Reviews were OK, but it was by no means greeted as Kane had been only five years earlier. "The Stranger is socko melodrama," wrote Variety, "spinning an intriguing web of thrills and chills. Director Orson Welles gives the production a fast, suspenseful development, drawing every advantage from the hard-hitting script from the Victor Trivas story. Plot moves forward at a relentless pace in depicting the hunt of the Allied Commission for Prosecution of Nazi War Criminals for a top Nazi who has removed all traces of his origin and is a professor in a New England school. Edward G. Robinson is the government man on his trail. Loretta Young is the New England girl who becomes the bride of the Nazi."

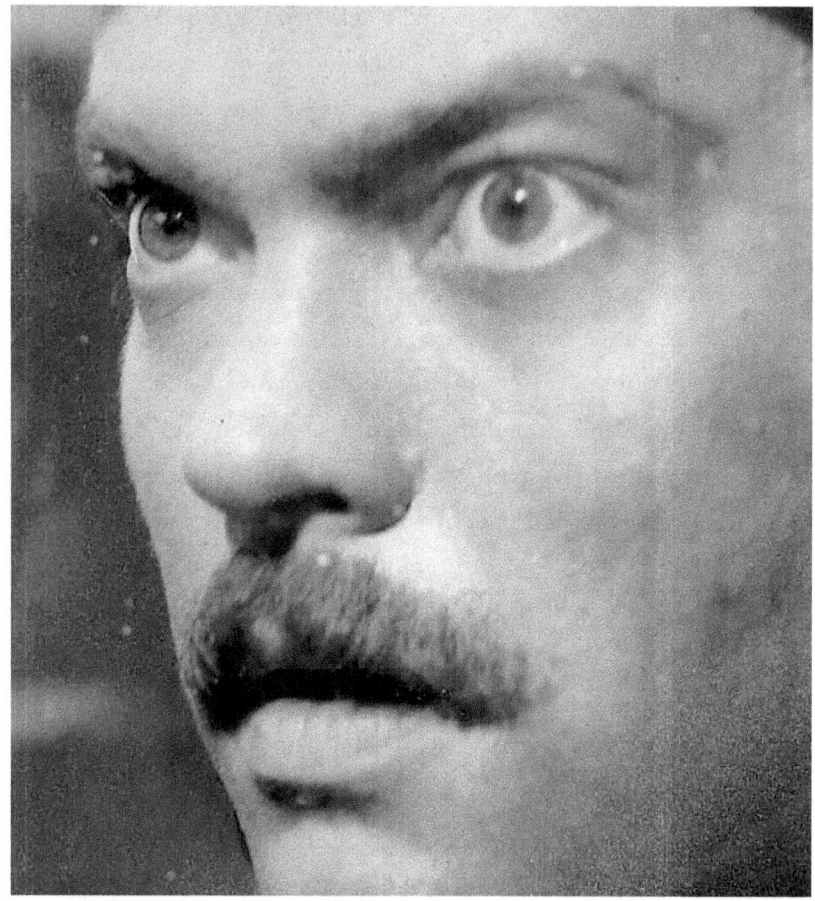

Orson Welles in The Stranger.

Financially however, the film was a hit, making three times its 1 million budget back in very little time. Clearly, Orson could make both high art and high entertainment, and as shown in The Stranger, could easily combine the two. For all this talk of Kane being a one off smash for Welles, The Stranger is a reminder that all those theories are nonsense. Clearly, the man knew how to deliver the goods, and could even shape a sub par idea or script into shape with a bit of hard work. For The Stranger, he removed his cloak of enigma and stepped up to do a professional job, playing the system and sticking to its rules. If he could craft such high art in such circumstances, it makes you wonder why he so often fought against the system, rather than attempting to function within it, with just a few mere compromises. But then again, how Wellesian would that have been?

A Room of Mirrors

In no time, he was on to another film project. In 1947 Welles took on the role of director for The Lady From Shanghai, quite simply, because he needed the money. At the time he was staging a theatre version of Around the World in 80 Days, but when producer Michael Todd pulled out, Welles required over 50,000 for costumes and financing. Somehow, Orson managed to convince head of Columbia, Harry Cohn, to provide the cash, upon the promise that Welles would write and direct a feature for them for free. There's a legendary story that goes with this tale, and it's one that has varied over the decades, depending on who told it. Somewhere in there lies the truth, but basically Welles claims to have picked The Lady From Shanghai (originally titled If I Die Before I Wake, written by Sherwood King) because it was the first book he saw in front of him.

"Overnight, he (Michael Todd) went bankrupt and I found myself in Boston on the day of the premiere," Orson later said, "unable to take my costumes from the station because 50,000 dollars was due.

Without that money we couldn't open. From Boston I got in touch with Harry Cohn, then director of Columbia, who was in Hollywood, and I said to him, 'I have an extraordinary story for you if you send me 50,000 dollars, by telegram in one hour, on account, and I will sign a contract to make it.' Cohn asked, 'What story?' I was telephoning from the theater box office; beside it was a pocket books display and I gave him the title of one of them: Lady from Shanghai.

I said to him, 'Buy the novel and I'll make the film.' An hour later we received the money. Later I read the book and it was horrible so I set myself, top speed, to write a story. I arrived in Hollywood to make the film with a very small budget and in six weeks of shooting. But I wanted more money for my theater."

The movie marked the only pairing of Welles and wife Rita Hayworth. The only problem was that Welles didn't want Hayworth for the lead. "At that time I was already separated from Rita; we were no longer even speaking. I did not intend to do a film with her," Orson said. But, as is the way in Hollywood, that's who ended up stepping up for the starring role. Though no longer in love, they clearly were both professional enough to get on with their jobs and make the best picture they could. "Cohn asked me why I didn't use Rita," Orson recalled. "She said she would be very pleased. I gave her to understand that the character was not a sympathetic one, and this might hurt her image as a star in the public eye. Rita was set on making this film, and instead of costing 350,000 dollars, it became a two million dollar film. Rita was very cooperative. The one who was horrified on seeing the film was Cohn."

In the film, Welles plays a sailor called Michael O'Hara, and Hayworth plays Elsa, who Welles saves when her horse coach is attacked by hooligans. He takes her home and discovers that she and her disabled attorney husband Arthur have just reached New York from Shanghai, but are soon on their way to San Francisco. Welles agrees to escort them on their journey, but ends up getting wrapped up in a fake murder plot with Arthur's partner George, played by Glenn Anders. So follows a typically murky, mysterious and captivating film noir tale with plenty of unexpected turns.

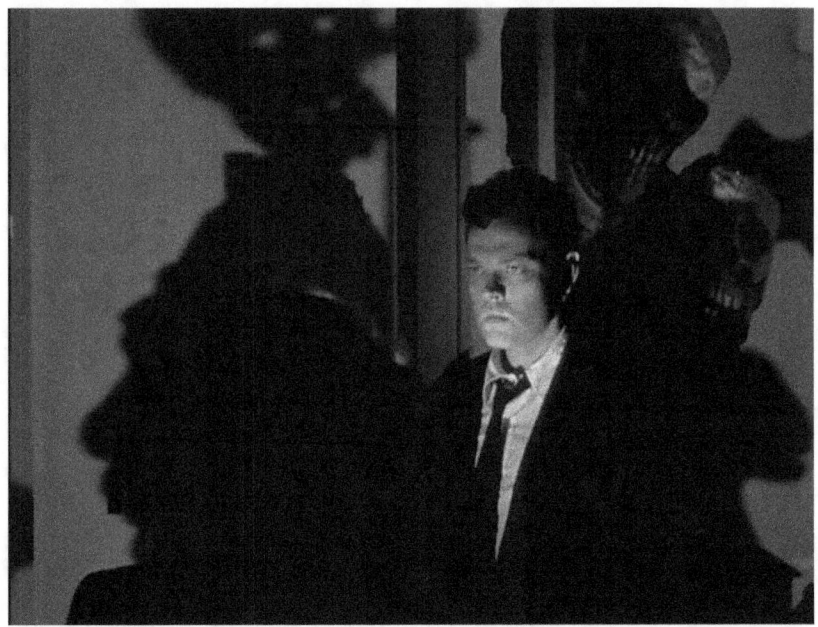

To say that Welles did this purely as a kind of bargain, he still put his all into the script and the execution of the high drama. Though he cut off her luscious long red locks, and made her crop it to a harsh short blond (devastating the studio and Cohn alike), he managed to get a very effective performance out of Hayworth, which for me is among her best work. Orson himself is subtly powerful too, in full 1940s iconic swing and unstoppable from start to finish. Though some of the enforced close ups of Hayworth are very sheen and Hollywood style (Orson was forced to go back in to shoot close ups by the studio, as they didn't feel there was enough starriness in the picture), the film is also very high art. The most breathtaking and memorable scene is undoubtedly the legendary funhouse mirror section, a dazzling and dizzyingly fantastic moment, which is among Welles' most intricate and excellently shot sequences.

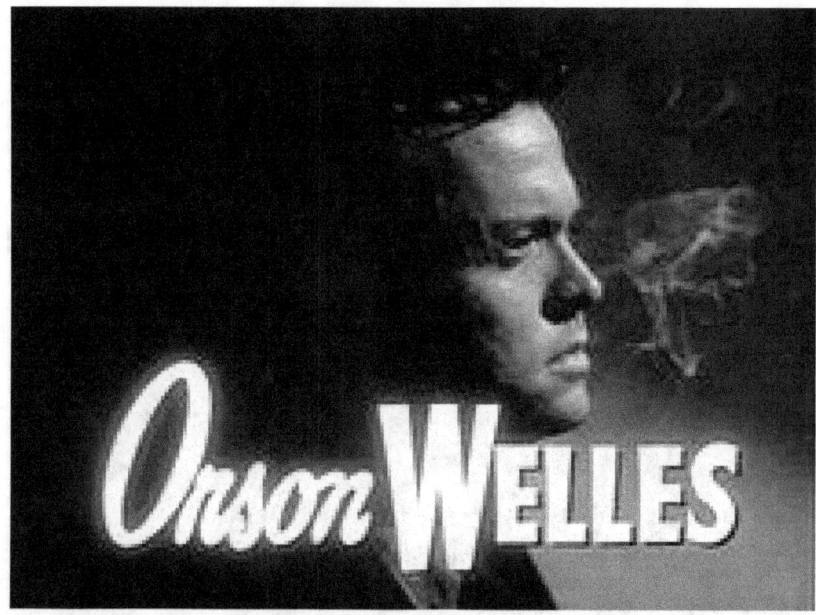

Of course, this being Orson, the making of the film was not a totally happy one. Denied his final cut of the picture, the one we all know and love is in fact a heavily edited version, betraying Welles' true vision. Again, he could not help but be disappointed. Yet as with Ambersons, the released cut is still a joy. But let's prey one day we might catch a glimpse of Orson's version, which will undoubtedly enter the film into his exclusive masterpiece category, currently inhibited by Kane and a handful of other pictures.

But reviews were not so good. New York Times slammed it, calling Welles and the film "ridiculous" and writing, "For a fellow who has as much talent with a camera as Orson Welles and whose powers of pictorial invention are as fluid and as forcible as his, this gentleman certainly has a strange way of marring his films with sloppiness which he seems to assume that his dazzling exhibitions of skill will camouflage. Take The Lady From Shanghai, for instance: it could have been a terrific piece of melodramatic romance. For the idea, at least, is a corker and the Wellesian ability to direct a good cast against fascinating backgrounds has never been better displayed. It's the story of a roving merchant seaman who falls in with some over-rich worldlings and who almost becomes the innocent victim of their murderous hates and jealousies. And for its sheer visual modelling of burning passions in faces, forms and attitudes, galvanized within picturesque surroundings, it might almost match Citizen Kane. As producer of the picture, Mr. Welles might better have fired himself— as author, that is—and hired somebody to give Mr. Welles, director, a better script. And he certainly could have done much better than use himself in the key role of the guileless merchant sailor who is taken in by a woman's winning charm. Mr. Welles simply hasn't the capacity to cut a romantic swath. Indeed, his performance in the picture—and his exhibitionistic cover-ups of the story's general untidiness—give ironic point to his first line: When I start out to make a fool of myself, there's very little that can stop me."

Clearly, Kane's success was something of a critical curse for Welles, who no matter what he achieved or strived for, could not measure up to its intimidating stature. The Lady from Shanghai, a perfectly good film, was a victim of his debut's smash success.

Retrospectively however it is seen as vintage Welles. Peter Bradshaw of the Guardian recently wrote, upon its re-release, "There's such outrageous brilliance in Orson Welles's brash and sexy noir melodrama from 1947, now on re-release. There are some opaque plot tangles, perhaps due to 60 minutes being cut from Welles's original version by the studio, but the sheer brio and style make it a thing of wonder, whisking the audience from the streets of New York City, to the open seas, to a tense courtroom and then to a bizarre house of mirrors. This is arguably Welles's best acting performance: theatrically romantic, with warmth, wit and a gust of pure charisma. It has an irresistible energy."

Welles Takes on Macbeth

In my humble view, no one brought the drama and beauty of Shakespeare to the screen quite like Orson Welles. Loading each picture with a threatening and imposing darkness, stunning visuals and perfect performances, Welles became the ultimate film adapter of the bard's work. The first Shakespeare work Welles tackled for the screen was Macbeth, easily the finest cinematic version of the often told story. He had of course brought it to the theatre in his revolutionary 1936 Federal Theatre production of the story. In that staging, he moved the location from Scotland to an island on the Caribbean, and employed a full African American cast to play the parts. The "voodoo Macbeth" went down in history and was hugely controversial in its time.

"There was a riot," Orson said in 1975, "and on the opening night the police were around, because there was a big part of the black community that thought we were making fun of them. So the police were there by hundreds, because the word had gone out that it was a kind of burlesque. But I spent a long time rehearsing... three months."

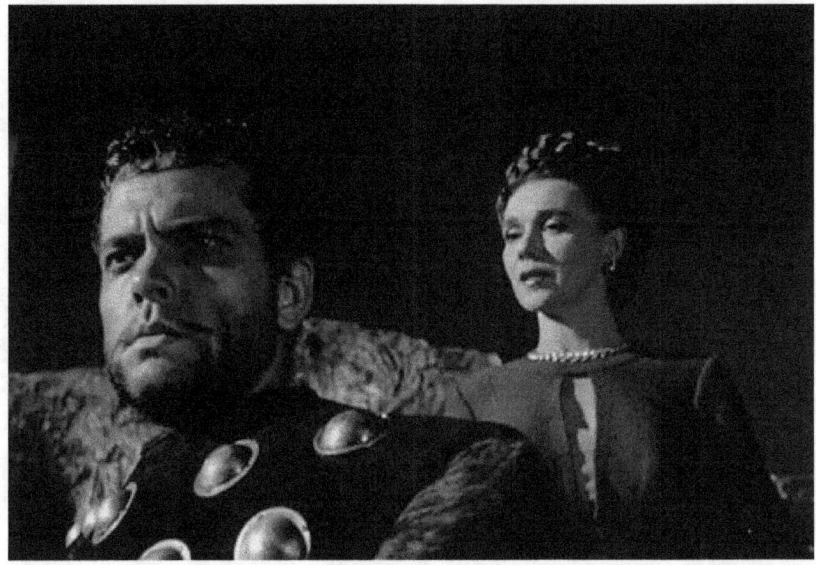

Over 11 years later, with Welles marriage to Hayworth over, he began cooking up ways to bring Shakespeare to life in the modern setting of the movies. He managed to get a deal with Republic Pictures, but the budget they provided was not of the sort he had previously been used to. Though only given $700,000, Orson agreed to personally cover any amount that went over the budget. Though he did not adopt any of the black or voodoo elements of his stage production, he did keep some of the darker aspects for the screen. He also added more scenes with the witches, to bring his vision into more Gothic horror territory.

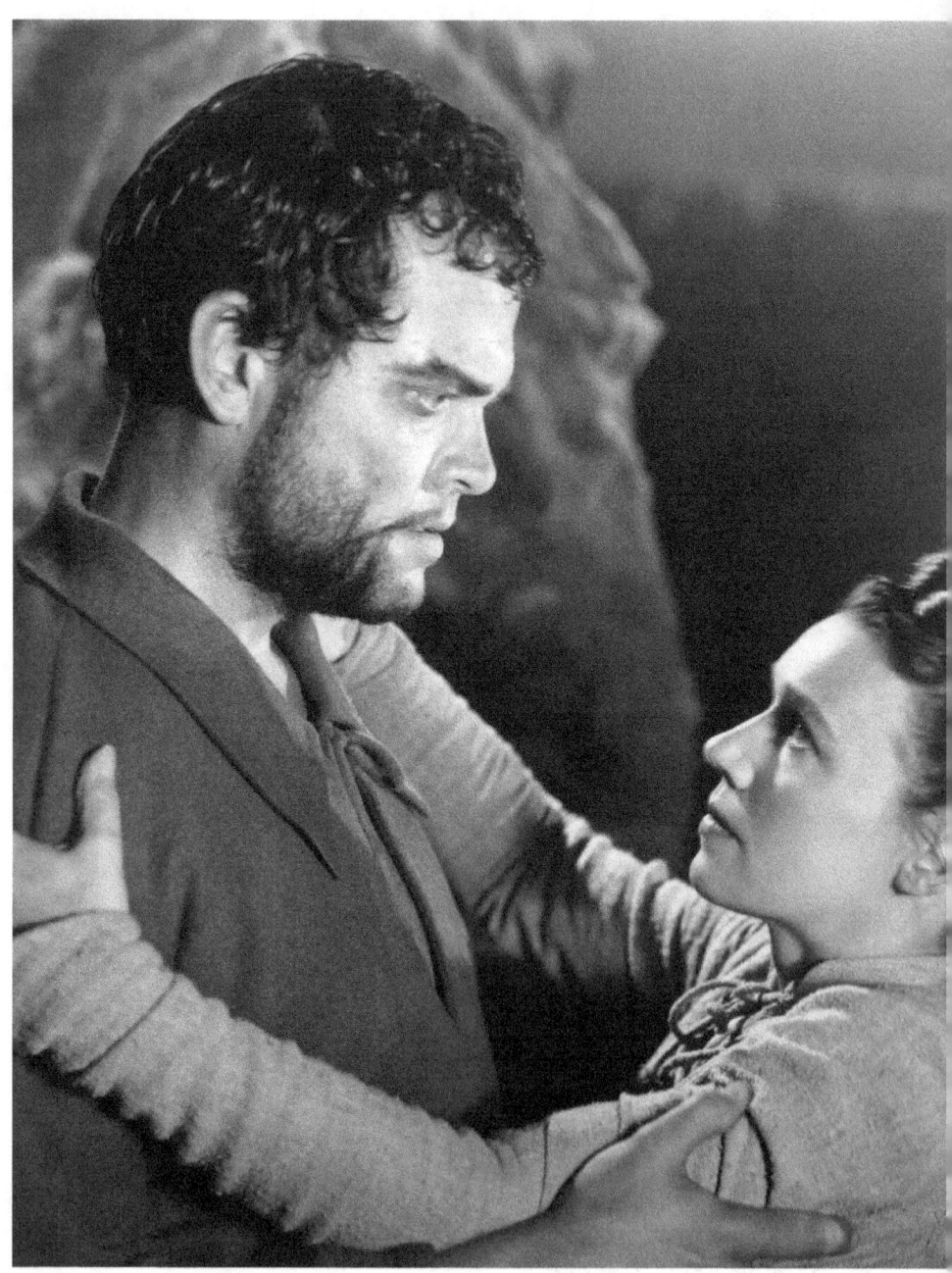

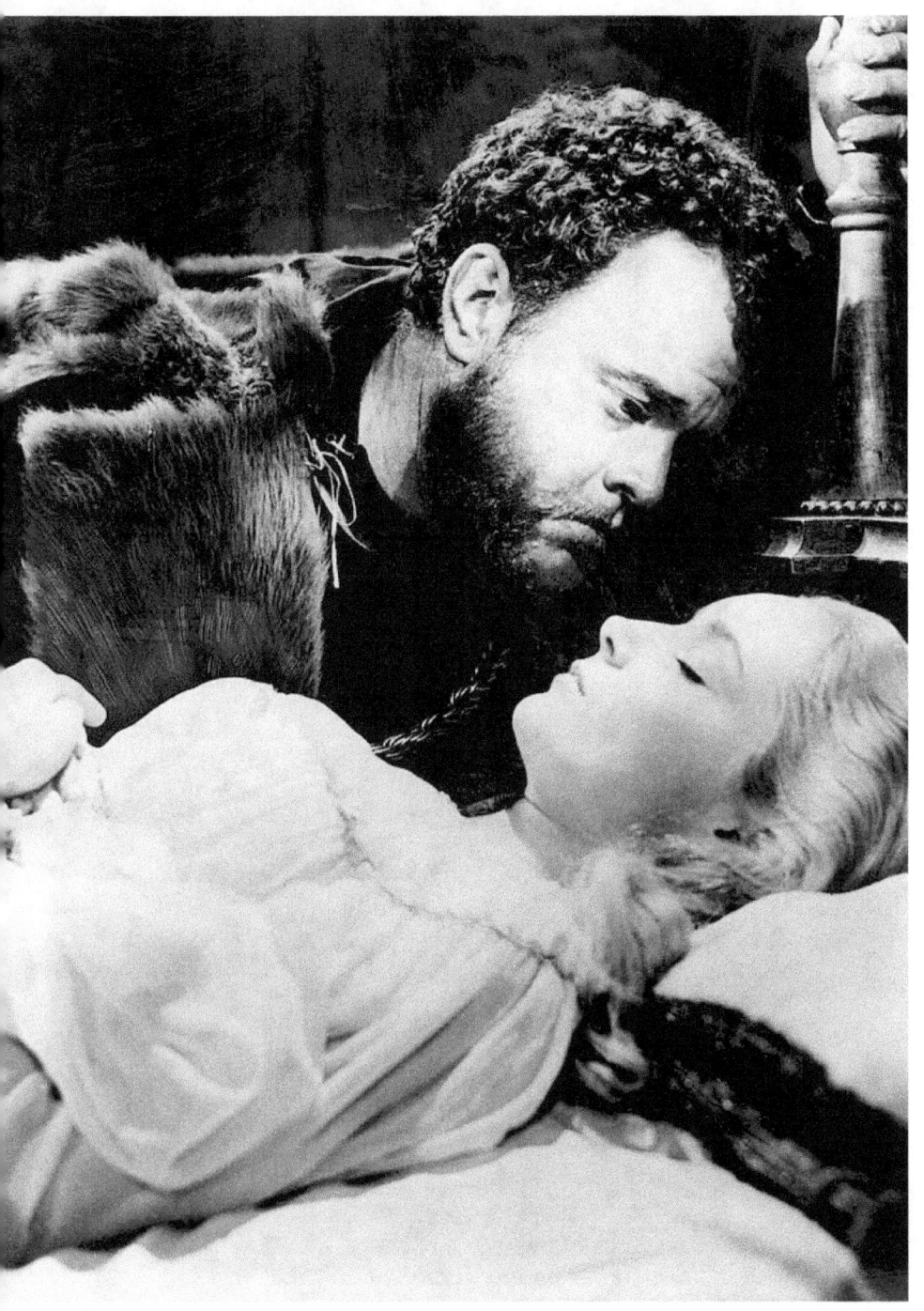

Othello (1951)

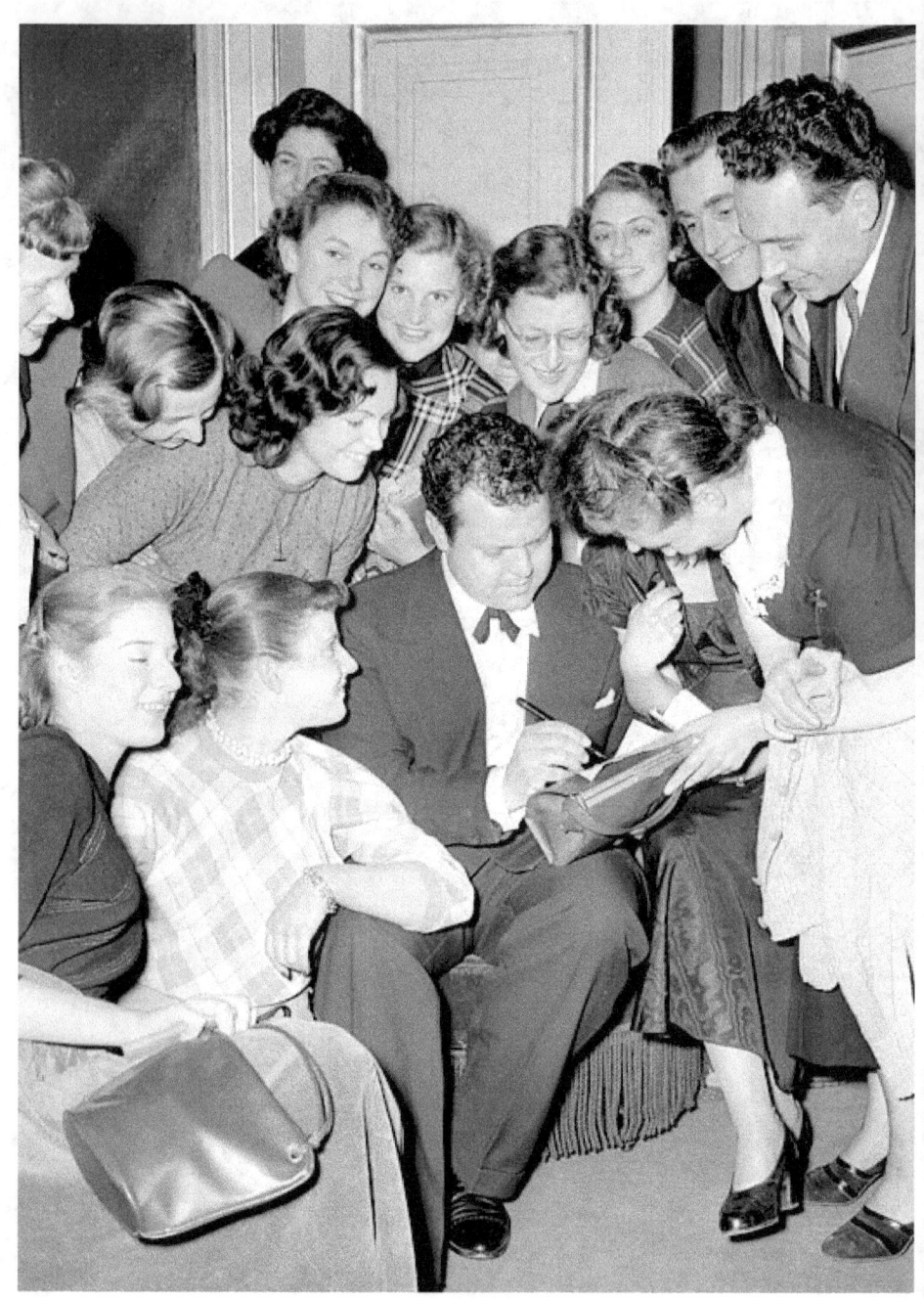

Welles signing autographs in 1952.

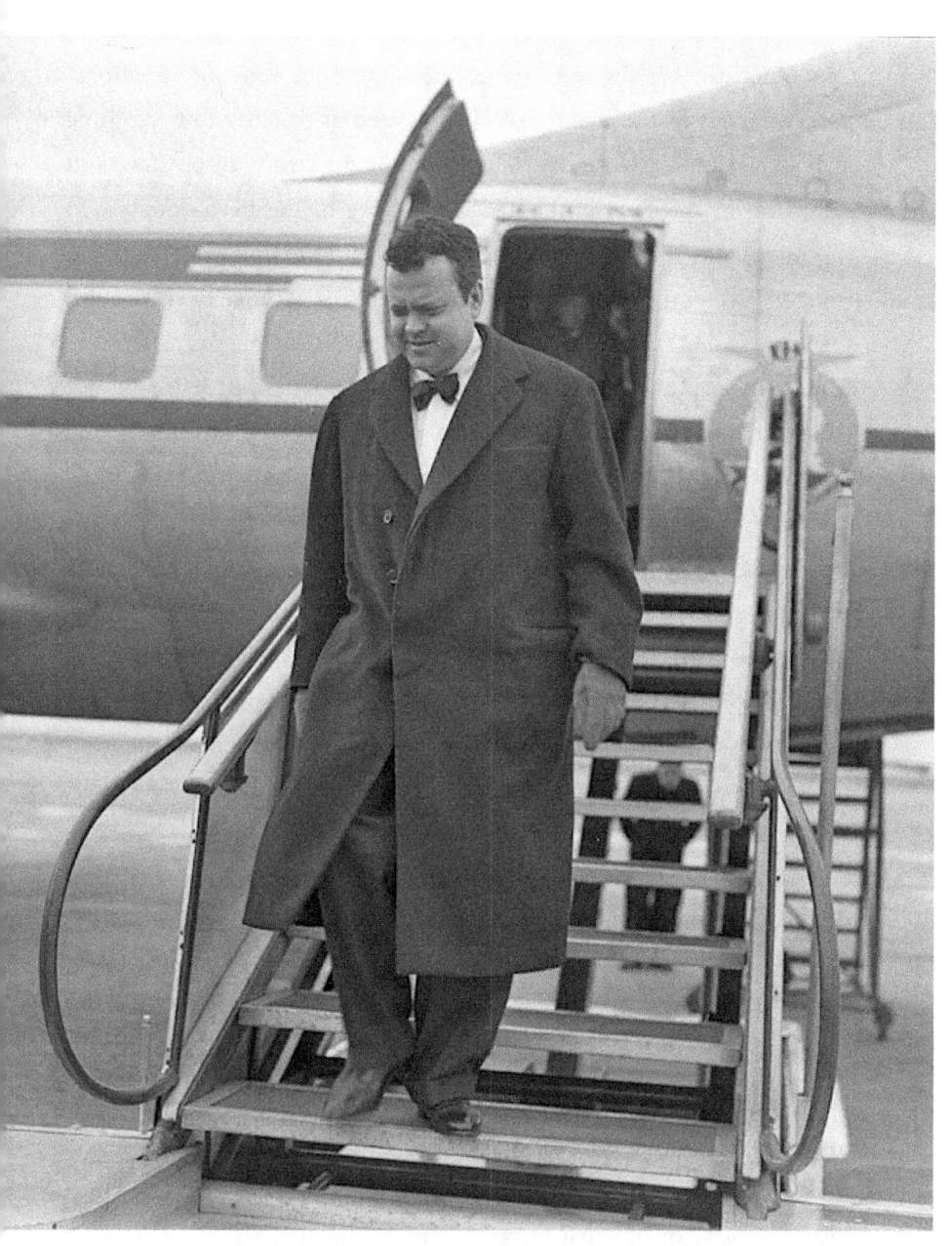

Orson touching down in Amsterdam, 1952.

As Macbeth, Welles puts in a stunning effort, one of the finest performances in the history of cinema, and as much a tour de force as his Charles Foster Kane. He commands the text with passion, and seems to have totally embodied every fibre of the hero's being. On top of this, as director, Welles executed some of his most dazzling imagery even on such a low budget, or perhaps because of it. Though the story is told briskly and with vitality, it's in the imagery where the film truly captures the depths of the imagination. The black and white cinematography by John L Russell is stark and striking, while one cannot shake off the silhouetted shots of the witches, as they cackle and mock, for hours after viewing. It is also the most unsettling, creepy and stunning Shakespeare adaption I have ever seen. On sheer filmmaking terms, and in the feelings it evokes, it is more than a match for Citizen Kane, in some ways more effective and arresting. Welles embodies the guilt and paranoia of the man, using thunderous music, atmospheric shots and the constant nagging of the crones to heighten the sense of fear.

"The forces of evil are trying to win him over," Welles later said, clearly impassioned by Macbeth's struggle with the dark side. "But the battle is not won at the beginning of the film, nor is it won at the end. Even at the end, Macbeth remains a member of the Christian world and continues to fight to save his integrity. The fact he is destroyed by evil doesn't mean that he is its plaything, as the forces of evil wanted him to be. Finally he falls, he collapses. His wife also uses him. Everyone uses him. It's the story of a weak man. This is why Macbeth has never been the great role for a great actor. To play it requires an actor of great physical and intellectual power, capable of incarnating a weakling. However you interpret Macbeth or the witches, Macbeth is a weakling. He's sick from the outset."

Welles brings every flaw and weakness to the character and makes him a multi dimensional being, rather than just a flat vessel for the blackness to have its way with. In bringing us inside the depths of the proceedings, we feel a part of the plot, in the thick of it, almost smelling the mud. Unsettling, stirring and utterly haunting, it remains one of Welles' crowning moments. The fact it was shot in only three weeks and on such a low budget makes the achievement even more admirable.

"Othello Was Orson Welles' Triumph!"

Three years after Macbeth, Welles would tackle another key Shakespeare work, the kind of towering work of literature that would fatefully intimidate and outface a lesser man. But Othello was one of his great goals, and if he could bring such cinematic power and originality to Macbeth, then he could no doubt achieve the same with Othello.

With Othello being such a long play, Welles had to shorten it for the screen. In fact he had to slice it in half and compress it down to a tidy 90 minutes. It marked one of the most chaotic and troublesome shoots Orson ever had, save for maybe one of his later unfinished works, like Other Side of the Wind. Shooting began in 1949, but the initial producer went bankrupt and funds dried up. When Welles began putting his own hard earned cash into the project (as he was to do time and time again later in his career), he soon found that he too was running out of money. So here and there, Orson would gather funds when he could, when he had acted in a third rate picture and got more money together.

The fact that Orson was able to salvage anything as good as he did from this shambolic shoot is a testament to his talents. In one interview, Orson even explained that he didn't always have the actors together for filming when needed, due to scheduling issues.

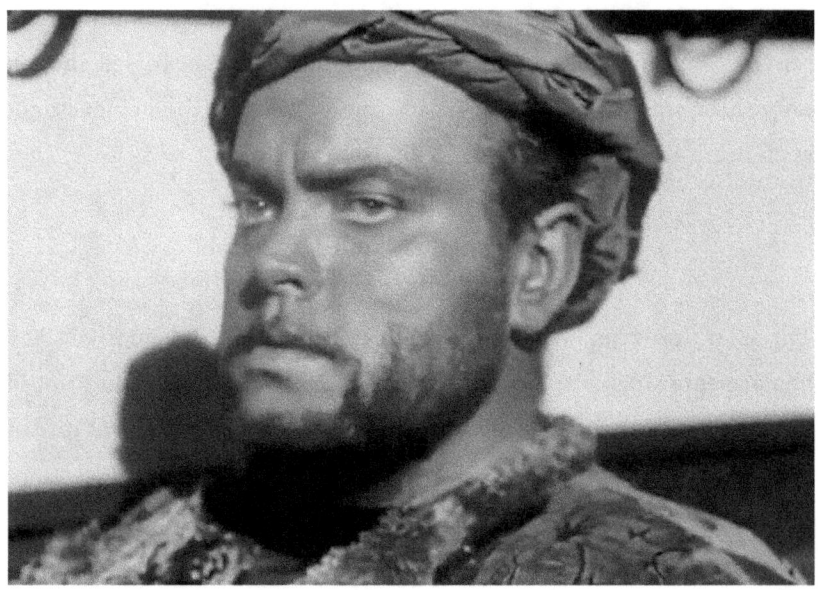

"I never had all the actors at the same time. Every time you see someone with their back turned, or with a hood on their head, you can be sure that it's a stand-in. So I had to do everything in shot, reverse-shot because I never managed to unite Iago, Desdemona Roderigo and others in front of the camera. But in Othello, too, the matches are very exact; I simply shot the film on different kinds of emulsions. The link shot can be as exact as possible, but if you shoot on Dupont, French Kodak, American Kodak and Ferrania, you have inevitably clashes in tonality when you mix them in the editing.

For Arkadin, again, I did not do long scenes because a long sequence requires a numerous and skilful crew: there are few European crews that have the men, the technicians capable of realizing a long sequence."

Orson did over see a 1951 edit of the film, but seven years after his death Beatrice Welles was involved in a new restoration of the film, with an extra million of funds spent on enhancing the quality. But for me, and many others in fact, the true version is Orson's, and it is, in retrospect, one of his most important works. It showed that if need be he could work independently and raise his own funds to see the film into completion. It's a pre cursor to his later years as kind of film outlaw existing on the outside of the mainstream. They say he was out of the system as an aging man, but the truth is, he was often skirting round the edges, even in the relatively early parts of his career.

The film has grown in reverence as the years have gone by. In France, it took years to get a release, but did very well over there. New York Times were among the publications who thought that Welles had triumphed in the visuals, but made an "unliterate" adaptation of a very literate tale. "And so this extraordinary picture, which it took more than three years to make and equally as long—or longer—to re-dub and prepare for showing here, is strictly an un-literate, inarticulate and hotly impressionistic film, full of pictorial pyrotechnics and sinister, shadowy moods. It would be hard to improve upon this rendering of Othello for sheer mise en scène. Mr. Welles has got Venice and Cyprus (or what passes for Cyprus) down to the ground. All the urbanity and stony beauty of the great Adriatic port and the island of Othello's triumph are made sharply visual in this film. But, alas for the import of the drama! It is mainly spectacle — elaborate, expensive, complicated—with no continuity, meaning or soul. Mr. Welles' own dusky Othello is a towering shadow of a man, monstrous in his pictorial movements but as hollow and heartless as a shell. There are flashes of brilliant suggestion in this tumbled, slurred and helter-skelter film. But they add up to nothing substantial — just a little Shakespeare and a lot of Welles."

Of course, this is just one man's vision of an immortal, historical piece of literature, but the interpretation just happens to be by Orson Welles. The man was a giant, and this remains one of his key works.

A Likeable Shambles...

Arkadin. Based on an episode of the radio series The Lives of Harry Lime, it's Orson clearly out of control. Not released in the US until the early 1960s, despite getting a 1955 release in Spain, it was one of the key factors in Orson's alienation from filmmaking. A heartbreaking experience for the great man, its one saving grace was in the fact it introduced him to his beloved Spain, which became his home for a number of years.

Yet over sixty years on, the film still looks good. It may be slightly disjointed, especially in regards to what Welles had in mind, but there is an enjoyment to be had. The biggest thrill of all is the appearance of Welles himself, as the extravagant and larger than life Gregory Arkadin. As in Kane, Welles aggrandises himself when his character's name is the last words uttered by a murdered man, rather like Rosebud being the final words of Charles Foster. It is Robert Arden's job to find Arkadin, a millionaire, and the whole adventure results in one of the most exciting climaxes in the whole of the Welles canon. It's all hammy fun, and certainly not his best work as a whole, but still extremely enjoyable.

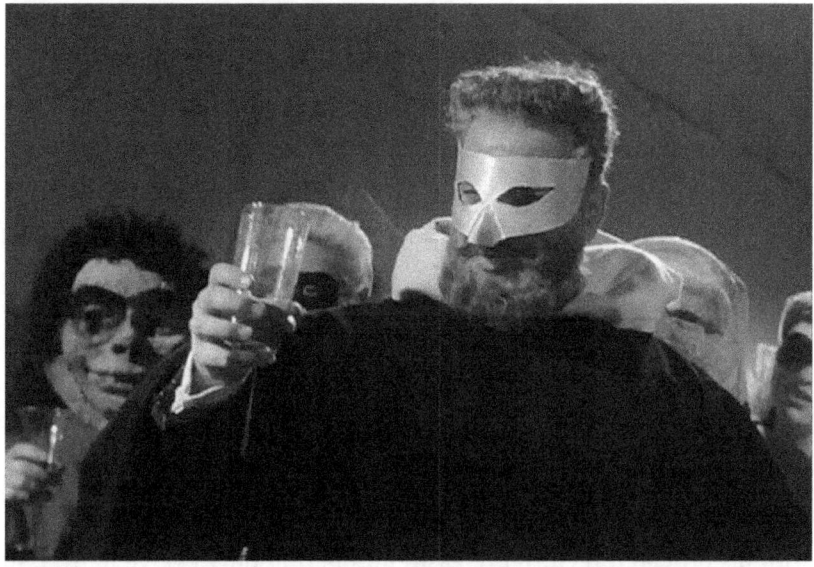

Typically, there are numerous prints and edits of the film, with Welles expert Jonathan Rosenbaum once getting it down to seven. However, the actual sum is now believed to be nine. Understandably, Welles called it the biggest disaster of his life, and it is perhaps the best, or worst, example of Welles exploitation and mistreating. Curiously, and as if to illustrate the lack of control he had over his work, there was also a tie in novel which was promoted as being written by Welles himself. However, Welles didn't have anything to do with it. "I didn't write one word of that novel," Welles told his friend Peter Bogdanovich. "Nor have I ever read it. Somebody wrote it in French to be published in serial form in the newspapers. You know

— to promote the picture. I don't know *how* it got under hardcovers, or who got paid for that."

Reviews were good at the time, but it failed to ignite as his earlier works had. Still, there were nice notices. "As an actor, he is as flamboyant as ever" raved the New York Times, "pouring out metaphors in his mellifluous voice and tilting formidably at the camera every time it swerves in his direction. His Arkadin is less a performance than a presence, and, on screen or off, it overwhelms a film, which, for all its strangeness, is seldom less than brilliant."

Retrospectively, the film has seen a resurgence of interest. Time Out wrote "Flamboyantly melodramatic, it's a playfully egocentric display of egocentrism and a magician's perverse revelation of his own trickery. Failure or not, it's irresistible."

Ian Dawe recently wrote an appraisal of the film for Sequart, concluding his piece with "Welles didn't make that many movies, with his official directorial releases numbering only twelve in over 40 years. But, like his fellow ex-patriot Stanley Kubrick, the ones he did make are all singular and worthy of attention. So, today, on Orson's birthday, treat yourself to a glass of wine, some frozen peas and discover Mr Arkadin."

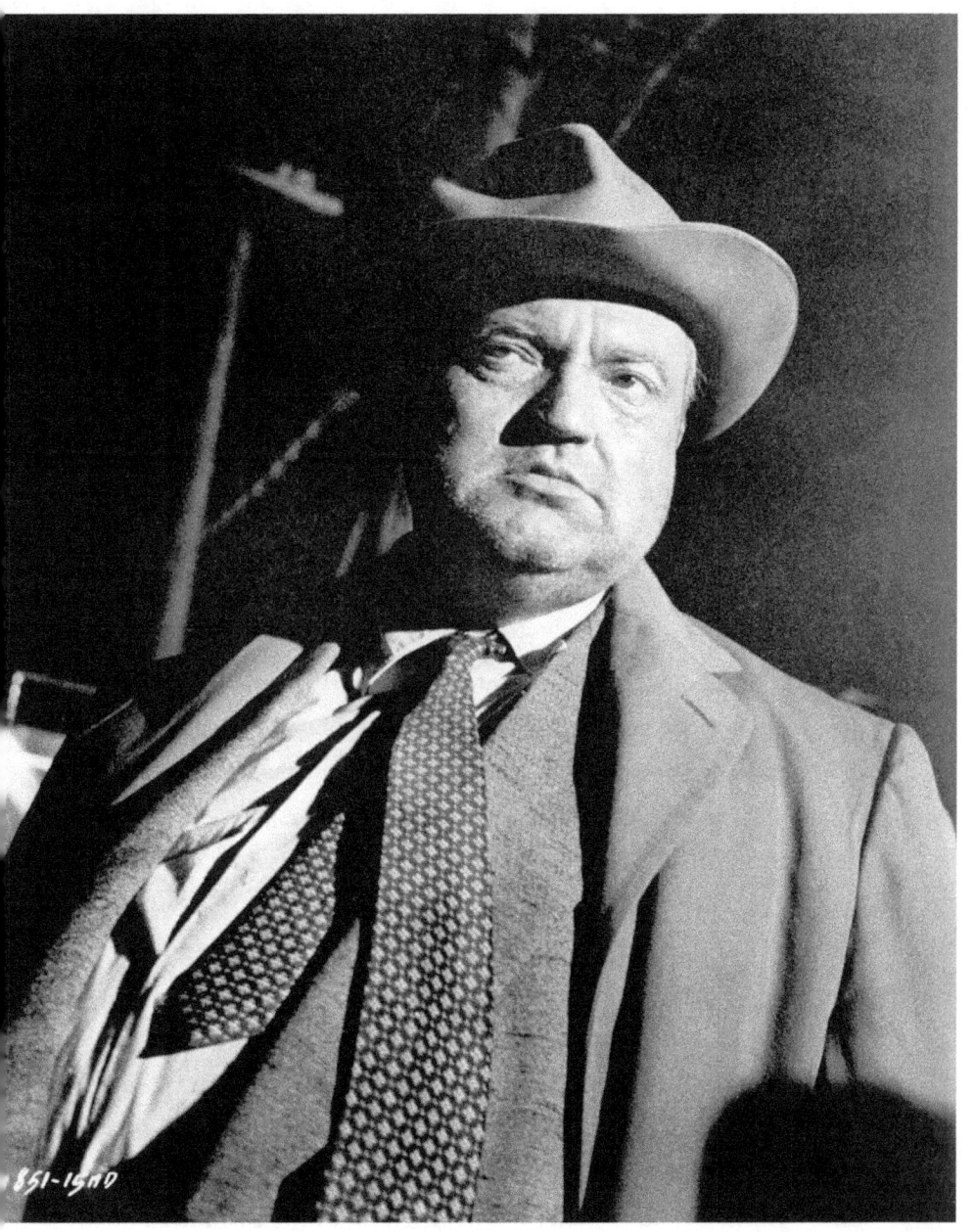

851-15AD

81

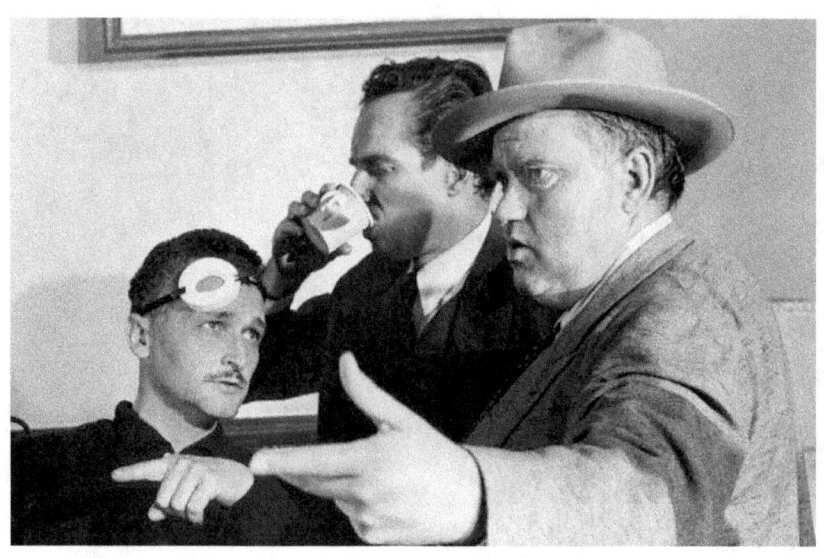

A Noir Masterpiece

"It's the eighth one!" Welles said at the time of the release of Touch of Evil, speaking of directing in general and keeping his integrity intact. "You know I've been working for seventeen years; I have directed eight films and I have edited only three of them. There are in this film (Touch of Evil) some scenes that I neither wrote nor directed, of which I know absolutely nothing. Or my style, for my vision of cinema, the editing is not one aspect, *it is the aspect.* Directing is an invention of people like you; it is not an art, or at most an art for a minute a day. This minute is terribly crucial, but it happens only very rarely. The only moment where one can exercise any control over a film is in the editing. But in the editing room, I work very slowly, which always unleashes the temper of the producers who snatch the film from my hands. I don't know why it takes me so much time: I could work forever on the editing of a film. For me, the strip of celluloid is put together like a musical score, and this execution is determined by the editing; just like a conductor interprets a piece of music in rubato, another will play it in a very dry and academic manner and a third will be very romantic, and so on. The images themselves are not sufficient: they are very important, but are only images. The essential is the length of each image, what follows each image: it is the very eloquence of the cinema that is constructed in the editing room."

Welles had suffered with the studios and he would suffer again, in very different ways admittedly. But for now he was able to work with a good cast on a strong story line. The next film Welles found himself directing turned out to be Touch of Evil, another classic noir tale featuring the man in a very showy, larger than life role. By far one of the most important, key works of Welles' career, it follows a winding tale of murder on the border of Mexico. Though Charlton Heston is the lead actor (he plays a drug enforcement official), Welles walks away with the picture in a truly blitzing part as police captain Hank Quinlan. He gets all the best scenes, and the most memorable dialogue, by far the most exciting member of the cast.

As had occurred before, Welles was originally just to be a member of the cast, but Heston claims to have put him forward as the best man for the directing job. According to other sources, in fact according to Welles himself, Orson apparently asked producer Albert Zugsmith for the worst script he had, as if to prove a point that he could make a fine film from a bad screenplay. A part of me wants to believe the latter tale, as it fits so well into Welles folk lore. To be honest though, it's probably Heston's more straight forward memory which is the truth.

During the shoot, Welles proved to be the very embodiment of the free and open "actor's director". Though he claimed it to be an overrated job, he also took great pride in his role as director, and established this story as a respectable piece of cinema, not some seedy B picture sleaze fest. Orson went all out to ensure there was never a dull moment in Touch of Evil. The female lead Janet Leigh, in her pre-Psycho days, later recalled the joys of working for the man on a good day. "It started with rehearsals. We rehearsed two weeks prior to shooting, which was unusual. We rewrote most of the dialogue, all of us, which was also unusual, and Mr. Welles always wanted our input. It was a collective effort, and there was such a surge of participation, of creativity, of energy. You could feel the pulse growing as we rehearsed. You felt you were inventing something as you went along. Mr. Welles wanted to seize every moment. He didn't want one bland moment. He made you feel you were involved in a wonderful event that was happening before your eyes."

"Charming is the wrong word," Heston said of Orson. "He was a charming man in his dinner conversation or something, but I don't mean he went around kissing the actors or anything. But he was very good with actors. He was very good with crewmen too. When he was directing the picture he would have you do what he wanted you to do, as would any director."

Happy with his work, Orson delivered Universal a rough cut of the film, under budget and within time. Welles was sure his career would now be back on track after a few missteps and clunkers, but then

Universal went and put it on a double bill with another picture. Worse still, it was ranked as a B picture, alongside the then higher profile, but now long forgotten, The Female Animal, which went out as the main presentation. Though ignored at the time by audiences, it is now one of the prime examples of classic 1950s film noir, and remains an undisputed classic.

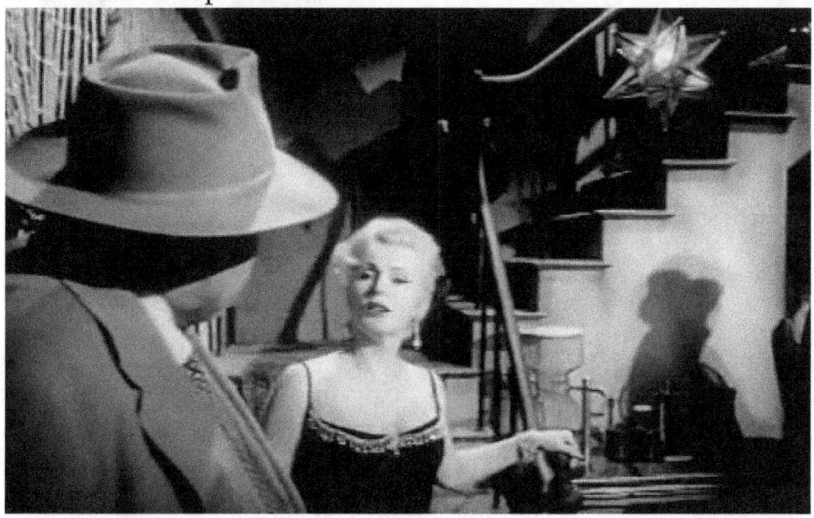

Still, some reviews at the time were ecstatic. The New York Times, who had been off Welles for a while, published a glowing notice. "Thanks to Orson Welles, nobody, and we mean nobody, will nap during Touch of Evil, which opened yesterday at R. K. O. theatres," they wrote. "Just try. The credits come on, for instance, to a sleepy, steady rumba rhythm as a convertible quietly plies the main street of a Mexican border town. The car is rigged with dynamite. And so, as a yarns-pinning director, is the extremely corpulent Mr. Welles, who co-stars with Charlton Heston and Janet Leigh in this Universal release. Any other competent director might have culled a pretty good, well-acted melodrama from such material, with the suspense dwindling as justice begins to triumph (as happens here). Mr. Welles' is an obvious but brilliant bag of tricks. Using a superlative camera (manned by Russell Metty) like a black-snake whip, he lashes the action right into the spectator's eye."

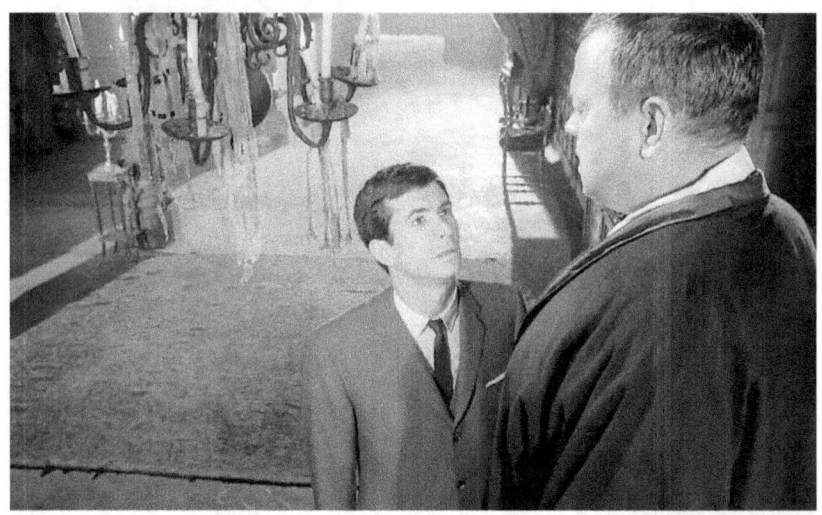

"That film of mine you hate..."
Welles and Kafka

Another film which at the time was underappreciated, but has grown in reverence over the years, is the Welles classic The Trial. Released in 1962, it was written and directed by Welles himself, adapted from the classic book by Frank Kafka. After a string of personally disappointing films for Orson, he felt like he had regained some of the grace and control he had enjoyed over twenty years earlier on Citizen Kane. Thanks in great part to this, The Trial remains a key work in his canon.

His fondness for The Trial was evident at the time too, when Huw Wheldon interviewed him for the BBC. "You know, this morning when I arrived on the train, I ran into Peter Ustinov and his new film, Billy Budd has just opened," Orson recalled. "I said to him, how do you feel about your film, do you like it? He said, I don't like it, I'm proud of it! I wish that I had his assurance and his reason for assurance, for I'm sure that is the right spirit in which to reply. I feel an immense gratitude for the opportunity to make it, and I can tell you that during the making of it, not with the cutting, because that's a terrible chore, but with the actual shooting of it, that was the happiest period of my entire life. So say what you like, but The Trial is the best film I have ever made."

In the same interview with Wheldon, Orson goes on to talk about the joy of seeing formerly low budget subject matter entering the mainstream, as well as his love affair with the cinema as an art form. "I don't think it would have been made five years ago, but if it had, it would only have gone to the art theaters and would have been made as a slender, difficult, experimental sort of film... Instead of being made as this is with Anthony Perkins, Jeanne Moreau, Romy Schneider-- you know, a big star cast, big picture! Imagine what that means, what it means for me to have had the chance to make it, indeed to have had the chance to work. This is the first job that I've gotten as a director in four years! That's my trouble! You see, if I'd only stayed in the theater, I could have worked steadily, without stopping for all these years. But, having made one film, I decided that it was the best and most beautiful form that I knew and one that I wanted to continue with. I was in love with it as you say, really tremendously so."

The film follows the tale of Anthony Perkins as Josef K, a man who we first see asleep in his room before he is dragged away and apparently held under arrest. Unaware of his crime, Josef K finds himself in a murky situation, involving law advocate Hastler, played imposingly by Orson Welles. What follows is a typically stunning Wellesian trip into confusion and mistrust, stylishly shot and taking in various technical and artistic innovations, all by the assured hands of Mr Welles.

That Welles saw it for some time as his finest film (he would later, in 1982 to the BBC, comment that 1965's Chimes of Midnight was his favourite of all his directorial movies) is no surprise. In every area the film succeeds; the performances are wonderful, particularly from Perkins, in what I believe is his finest on screen effort, aside his iconic Norman Bates; and the great Jeanne Moreau is wonderful too as Perkins' neighbour. Still, it's somehow Orson who manages to walk away with the picture, charisma personified here in one of his defining roles.

The whole project had originally come about when producer Alexander Salking approached Welles with the offer of making a film adaptation of any public domain work he might like. Welles chose The Trial, even though it turned out not to be in the public domain at all (a typical Welles story). Making considerable changes to the script, he didn't see it as much a film based on the book, or even an interpretation of it. He thought a film was a totally separate entity to a book, and neither two forms should be compared in any way. Thus, Welles inserted a lot of black humour into it, and at one point told Perkins it was indeed intended to be a black comedy.

Anyone surprised by this need only watch the picture again, as it's so obviously comedic in tone, especially in the interrogation scenes.

Roger Ebert later wrote a rave review of the film. "I was once involved in a project to persuade Orson Welles to record a commentary track for Citizen Kane. Seemed like a good idea, but not to the Great One, who rumbled that he had made a great many films other than Kane and was tired of talking about it. One he might have talked about was The Trial, his version of the Franz Kafka story about a man accused of--something, he knows not what." Giving it four out of four, Ebert also saw it as symbolic to Welles' situation, writing that one must "see it as autobiographical. After Citizen Kane and The Magnificent Ambersons, Welles seldom found the freedom to make films when and how he desired. His life became a wandering from one place to another. Beautiful women rotated through his beds. He was reduced to a supplicant who begged financing from wealthy but maddening men. He was never able to find out exactly what crime he'd committed that made him "unbankable" in Hollywood. Because Welles plays the Advocate, there is a tendency to think the character is inspired by him, but I can think of another suspect: Alexander Salkind, producer of The Trial and much later of the Superman movies, who like the Advocate, liked people to beg for money and power that, in fact, he did not always have."

Though it doesn't immediately spring to mind when one thinks of Welles the auteur, it is slowly building its own reputation as an essential part in Orson's cinematic canon. Fans of the film should seek out the unfinished but readily available documentary Filming The Trial, where the great man takes part in a Q and A at the University of Southern California about the making of the film.

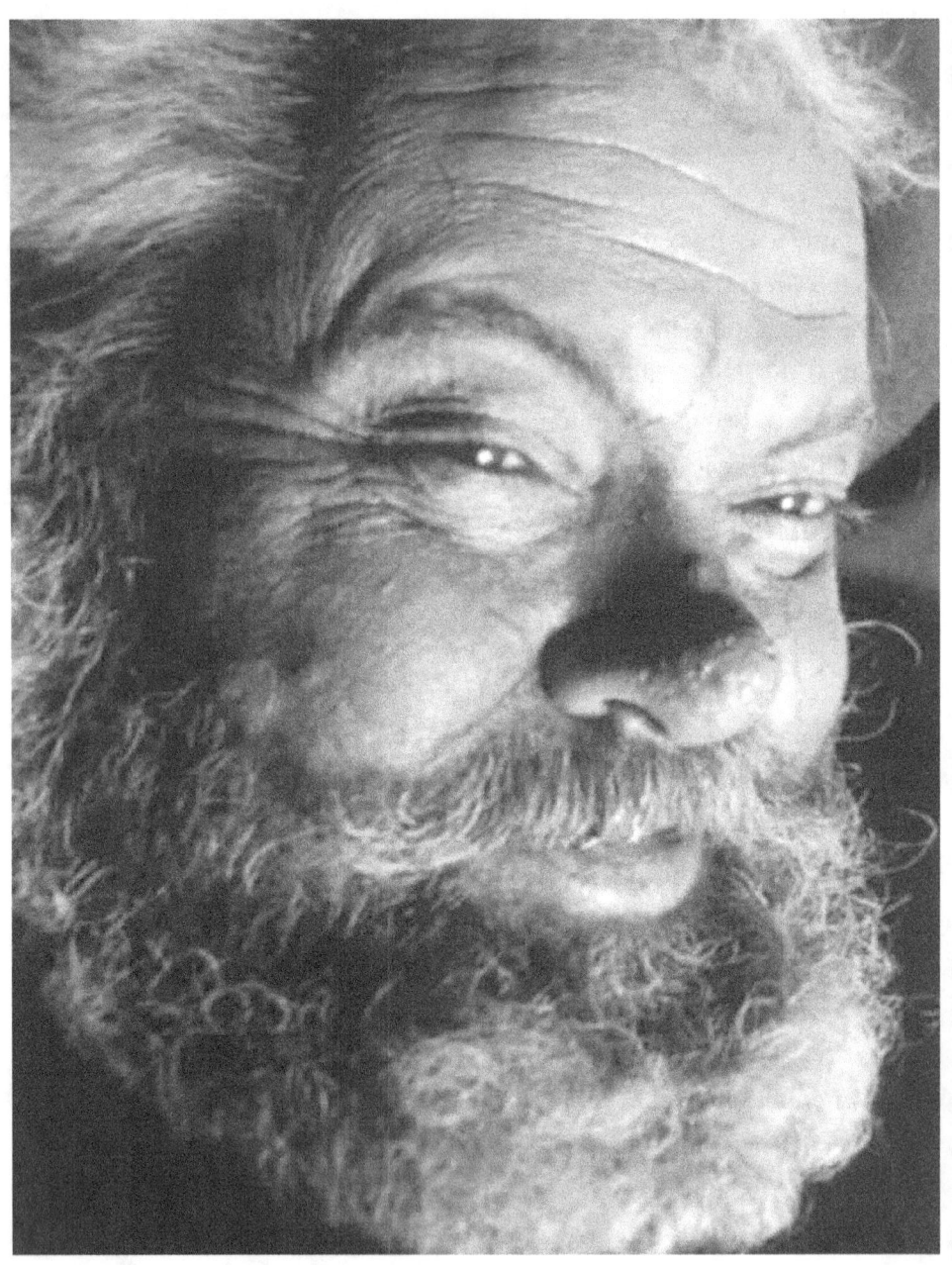

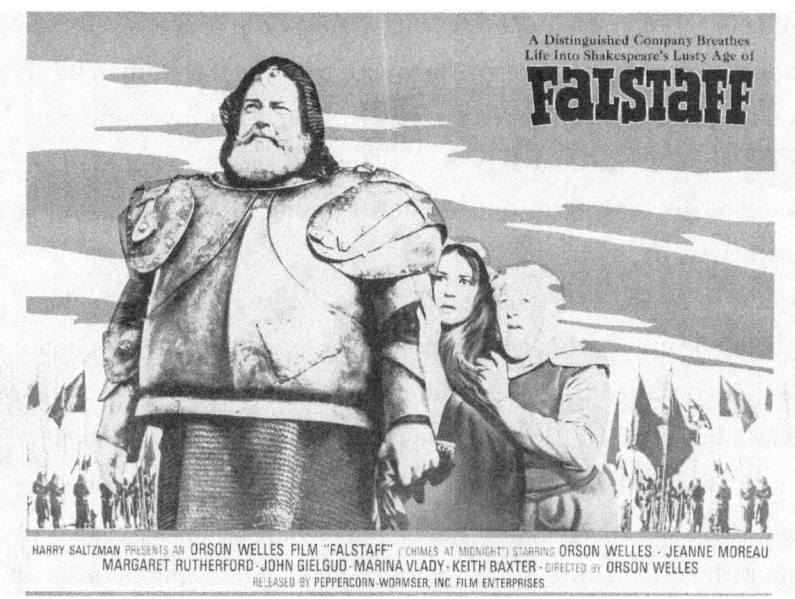

A Distinguished Company Breathes Life Into Shakespeare's Lusty Age of

FALSTAFF

HARRY SALTZMAN PRESENTS AN ORSON WELLES FILM "FALSTAFF" ("CHIMES AT MIDNIGHT") STARRING ORSON WELLES · JEANNE MOREAU
MARGARET RUTHERFORD · JOHN GIELGUD · MARINA VLADY · KEITH BAXTER · DIRECTED BY ORSON WELLES
RELEASED BY PEPPERCORN-WORMSER, INC. FILM ENTERPRISES

"The least flawed..."

Though Orson would rank Chimes At Midnight as the best film he ever directed, he wasn't going to totally pat himself on the back. He called it "the least flawed" of his movies, and in Orson's perfectionist vision, that's a pretty good summarisation. Chimes At Midnight is, as far as I can see, a flawless picture, a dazzling, low budget experience and a prime example of Orson not burning out after Citizen Kane. Anyone digging deep into his career, and not quite believing the often told tale of the man who never matched his debut, will no doubt be delighted by the charms of Chimes at Midnight. I know I was.

"It was successful for what I tried to do," Orson told the BBC, "I succeeded more completely in my view with that than with anything else." This, coming from Welles, is high self praise, but the fact he could not just come and out say what a great little film it is tells you something about his modesty. This is not false modesty either, this is genuine. Personally, I think it's up there with, if not more enjoyable than, Citizen Kane, and fifty odd years on since its inception, its reputation is only growing - slowly mind you, but growing nonetheless.

Welles' take on Shakespeare's Falstaff is, for me, possibly the finest character he ever portrayed on screen, a large, jovial, fun loving man; and though flawed to some (although not to Orson), a joy to watch. Welles himself called Falstaff "the most unusual figure in fiction, in that he is almost entirely a good man. A gloriously life affirming good man, and there are few gigantic silhouettes on the horizon of fiction who are good. They are always flawed, interesting because of what is wrong with them. Someone once said that Falstaff was the Hamlet who stayed in England and got fat. It's very amusing, but it's not true. Hamlet is not a good man. There is hardly a good man in literature. I think Shakespeare was greatly preoccupied, as I am in my humble way, with the loss of innocence. And I think there has been in England, an older England which was sweeter and purer, the weather was always spring time... the gentle warm breezes. You feel the nostalgia for it. You feel it also in Shakespeare. He was profoundly against the modern age as I am."

Welles' obsession, or perhaps love, for Chimes At Midnight went all the way back to 1930 when he was still at school in Woodstock, Illinois. Playing Richard III in a three hour play, he tried to group together several of Shakespeare's plays, but was made to cut down his presentation. Nearly ten years on, he staged a play called Five Kings with the Mercury Theatre players, another adaptation of several

Shakespeare works, handled more successfully. Twenty years later in 1960, Welles finally staged Chimes At Midnight in its known form in Ireland, with more passion and emphasis on Falstaff and his relationship with Hal. Unfortunately, poor turn outs caused Welles and Hilton Edwards to cancel the project.

When the film went into production in 1964, only Orson and his daughter Beatrice remained from the stage version. Welles made a deal with Spanish producer Emiliano Piedra, who only agreed to fund the film under the stipulation that they simultaneously work on a film version of Treasure Island. Little did Piedra know that Orson had no intention to make Treasure Island, and only said he would so the producer would go ahead with Chimes At Midnight.

Shot on a budget of 800,000, Welles and his cast and crew had to be very careful with money to say the least. By being economical and using clever filming techniques, Welles ensured Chimes At Midnight looked and felt like a big budget extravaganza, despite the fact it was anything but. Shot in Spain between late 64 and mid 65, Welles later joked how sad and pathetic the start of certain takes would have looked without the editing, commenting on a lot of "poor gypsies turning to the camera wondering when they were going to be fed." Again, Welles was able to laugh at the way the film industry had side lined him, to the point he was using doubles to pose for the backs of big name actors who could only be afforded for a matter of days (John Geilgud was present for ten days, Jeanne Moreau for five) or if he was lucky, weeks, in the case of Margaret Rutherford. Whenever he ran out of money, he would break off to gather more funds, while other scenes had to be cut for practicality.

The pace and feel of Chimes At Midnight is utterly frantic, and though there are some creaky overdubs, there is a level of urgency and excitement which keeps the dialogue and well played characterisations fresh. As Falstaff, Welles towers above the rest of the cast, both physically and in sheer terms of pure charisma. Anyone fond of Orson being left to his own devices and ripping through some of the best writing of all the ages will have a field day with this. I could literally watch hours of Orson as Falstaff, for me the ultimate embodiment of an actor high on glee and creative freedom.

Though the film was a rave at Cannes Film Festival upon its 1966 premier, it received enough poor reviews so that the distributor Harry Saltzman panicked and snuck it out to only a handful of theatres. Some of the reviews were very harsh, with Time writing that Welles was too fat to play Falstaff, taking commands of scenes "less with spoken English than body English." Others loved it though, and years on it's developed quite a reputation. As recently as 2012, it was ranked in the ten best films of all time by directors for BFI's Sight and Sound Magazine.

"How can it be that there is an Orson Welles masterpiece that remains all but unseen?" Roger Ebert wrote in 2006. "I refer not to incomplete or abandoned projects that have gathered legends, but to Chimes at Midnight, his film about Falstaff, which has survived in acceptable prints and is ripe for restoration. I saw the film in early 1968, put it on my list of that year's best films, saw it again on 16mm in a Welles class I taught, and then could not see it for 35 years. This is a magnificent film, clearly among Welles' greatest work, joining Citizen Kane, The Magnificent Ambersons, Touch of Evil and (I would argue) The Trial. It is also magnificent Shakespeare, focusing on Falstaff through the two Henry IV plays to his offstage death in Henry V. Although the plays are much abridged, it is said there is not a word in the film not written by Shakespeare. Welles was born to play Falstaff, not only because of the physical similarity but because of the rich voice, sonorous and amused, and the shared life experience. Both men lived long and too well, were at odds with the powers at court and were constantly in debt. Both knew disappointment, and one of the most sublime moments in Welles' career is simply the expression on his face at the coronation of Henry V, when he cries out God save thee, my sweet boy, and the new king replies, I know thee not, old man."

A stunning feat, even for Orson, and one of the most breathtaking performances in the history of modern cinema.

The Immortal Story: A Buried Gem

Possibly the most unfairly sidelined of Orson's directorial films, Welles' adaptation of Karen Blixen's short story The Immortal Story is a sublime, wonderful and simply beautiful experience, which thankfully is starting to get the credit it truly deserves. The first movie he directed in colour, The Immortal Story is visually stunning, and among his finest works, even though at a mere 60 minutes, it's also among his shortest.

As Mr Charles Clay, Welles is a marvel to be seen, embodying the lonely merchant getting closer to death by the minute. When he and his friend Levinsky (Roger Coggio) discuss a much told urban tale about an old man who gives five guineas to a sailor to impregnate his wife, Clay becomes obsessed and wants to make the tale come true.

He then sends Levinsky off to find both the sailor and the woman who will fill the role of the impregnated girl.

Clay is the very definition of an unfulfilled old man looking to see his wildest fantasies acted out before him, nearing death's door and smelling the scent of his own impending demise, but still desperately fighting the harshness of reality, and the contrast between the romantic and the realistic. In his various costumes, Welles looks to be relishing the chance to shine in one of his most subtle efforts.

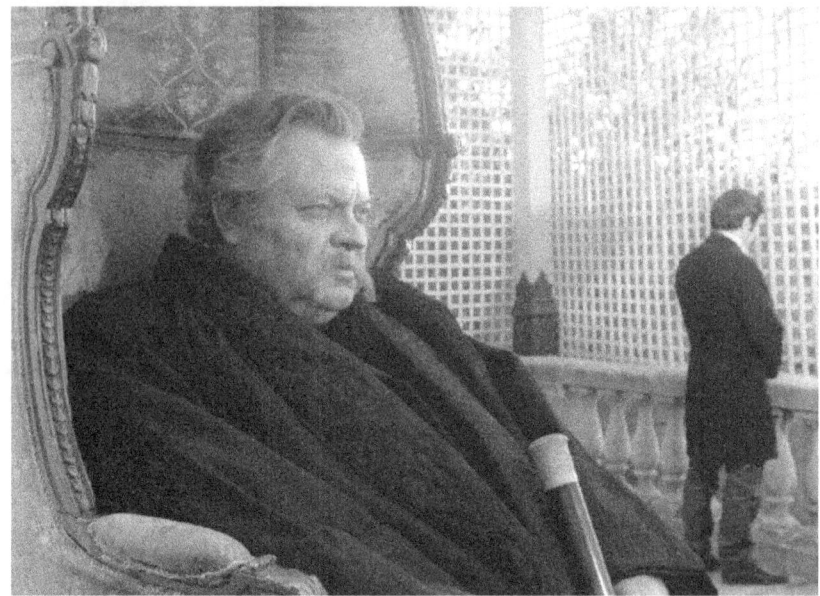

It is also clear what a fan he was of Blixen's work. Though he wanted to make a series of movies based on her works, Orson decided to focus on The Immortal Story solely, which he first intended to make as a two parter before condensing it into a neat 60 minutes. The decision for the movie to be in colour was not a personal choice for Welles. It was in fact his funders who insisted on colour, as Welles was famously not a fan of it. He much preferred black and white, seeing it as classier and more suited to actors, claiming colour distracted the viewer too much from the performances. Coming from a man who grew up seeing the films of the thirties, one can see his point. But funnily enough, The Immortal Story works brilliantly in colour, and it's the varied shades where the film finds much of its haunting dreaminess. Even if you believe black and white cinematography might have heightened the film's surreal aspects, one cannot help but soak up every bright and dim colour alike.

For me, as rich as the direction and cinematography may be, it's in Orson's wonderful performance where the true gold is, a man who is so alone and cut off from the outside world in his expansive mansion that he is almost like a counterpoint to Charles Foster Kane. But in many ways this is a more assured performance, and the film it sits comfortably within is more compact and direct. That's not to say it is "better" than the much revered Citizen Kane, but there are certainly aspects to The Immortal Story which elevate it towards prime Welles magic.

When I watched the film for the first time I could not help but feel that somehow Clay is some kind of Welles alter ego, or an observation on the more voyeuristic aspects of the filmmaker. In insisting that the often told myth be acted out before him, Welles' Clay is like a filmmaker who wants the show to unfold in front of his eyes. It makes you question the needs of the film director, and why he would so want to stage events as he does. With my theory in mind, I was pleased to discover that Peter Bogdanovich also observed this metaphor, and even put it to Welles himself in one of their legendary interviews. Orson refused to go along with Peter's image of Clay though and insisted that Clay was merely playing God, not some kind of perverse allegory of a filmmaker. But when Welles added that Clay indeed dies of disappointment, this aging millionaire magnified certain dissatisfied aspects of the real Orson Welles. Was Orson a man so saddened by his own cinematic misadventures and failed projects, that he too felt he could literally die of disappointment if any more of his dream films were scraped into the bin before the cameras even began rolling? Maybe it's too far fetched, and Welles himself might have slapped me down for such pontificating.

Notices for the film have been good over the years, though few have been on the level of what I believe it truly deserves. Time Out wrote, "Though shot for television on a low budget, this is a sumptuous experience, a fairytale-like story... Basically, it's about the conflict between the cold-blooded realism of the merchant and a romanticism he refuses to accept; and inevitably, the myth turns upon him. Welles is his usual megalomaniacal self, and the use of deep focus, deep shadow and colour is superb. The material itself is fascinating, and Erik Satie's music is perfectly chosen."

Slant Magazine were one of the publications who saw the clear similarities between Clay and Welles, as indeed most would when taking in the poetic darkness and strange beauty of this hazy story. "When Clay dies, he drops a large seashell while sitting in a throne, which brings to mind Charles Foster Kane, in Citizen Kane," Slant noted, "dropping a snow globe as he himself dies. Whether Welles intended it or not, The Immortal Story has autobiographical weight, as it's a film about storytelling that doubles back on the thematic and formal significance of everything Welles created prior to it, just as Clay doubles back on his own life. Though he loathed this sort of interpretation of his career, Welles is ultimately indistinguishable from Clay, as both are simultaneous termites and pioneers."

Anyone who really believes Welles was a spent force by the late sixties (or for that matter, even earlier than that) need only take another look at The Immortal Story, which is enthralling from the very first frame to the last. Mini, condensed and full of unforgettable imagery, it exists as one of his finest works. In the midst of odd ball cameo roles, documentary narration and work done purely for the money alone, the last fully fiction film of one of film's greatest ever figures deserves legendary status. The recent Criterion Collection DVD shows that it may perhaps achieve that someday.

Norman Eshley, who plays the sailor, recently shared his memories with me about working for Welles on the film:

"I played the lead in the Bristol Old Vic's showcase play in 1966 and I joined the Old Vic company to tour the USA with three plays. My agent rang me and sent me to London for an audition. I never asked what it was for, did it and went back to Bristol. I then had another call from my agent who said "Orson Welles wants to see you in Madrid". I was astonished to say the least. The tickets arrived and Mum and Dad took me to Heathrow. It was the first time I had flown.

At Madrid airport I was met by a man with a stretch limo and I was driven to Welles' house. I was met by Welles wife, Paola, who told me that Orson was delayed because he had been out getting drunk with Joseph Cotton and was sleeping it off.

Later that afternoon I was called into the house and waited in Orson's study. The great man arrived. I was warned by his staff that he didn't like yes-men so I argued with him about a playwright of whom I knew almost nothing. He realised that I was bluffing and started to laugh. He pressed a bell on his desk and his secretary came in. "Give the guy some dough and let him go see the town". I said goodbye to Welles and was taken outside. "You've got the job" I was told. I went home still not knowing what the job was.

Welles had me on set in costume for about a week before he used me. He knew that it was my first role and that I knew nothing about filming. In those days drama schools only taught stagecraft. He wanted me to learn on the set and it was invaluable. We had lunch together every day and I began to understand the process. Then one day he said that I would be filming the next day. So my first day's professional work was in bed with Jeanne Moreau directed by Orson Welles!

He was nothing but kindness towards me and I feel strange saying Orson because I never called him anything but Mr Welles. The very fact that I had his name on my CV opened all sort of doors. Some 20 years after the film I was employed by directors wanting to know about him. My memories are of a very kind giant that kicked off my career."

The Making and Unmaking Of A Genre

One of the most famous Orson projects from the latter period was his masterpiece F For Fake, a film essay and documentary which focused on the great forger Elmyr de Hory. Of course, with this being Welles, a straight forward visual investigation was never going to be enough. So Orson shook the formula about. One half of the film was pure documentary, while the other half redefined what it was to make a study of an individual and his chosen profession, in this case a famous fake. Putting in scenes of his exotic looking girlfriend Oja Kodar, himself, and the great famed hoax writer Clifford Irving, F For Fake introduced a new genre. At the time, it was side lined and Orson found it hard to distribute his unorthodox film. Now however, it's a masterpiece. Though he had gone in a similar direction in the earlier Portrait of Gina for TV, this was fresh. The big twist was in the fact that we the viewer of this study of fakery could not even trust the filmmaker. It was a brave move, and few, if any, have ever attempted anything so brave and challenging since.

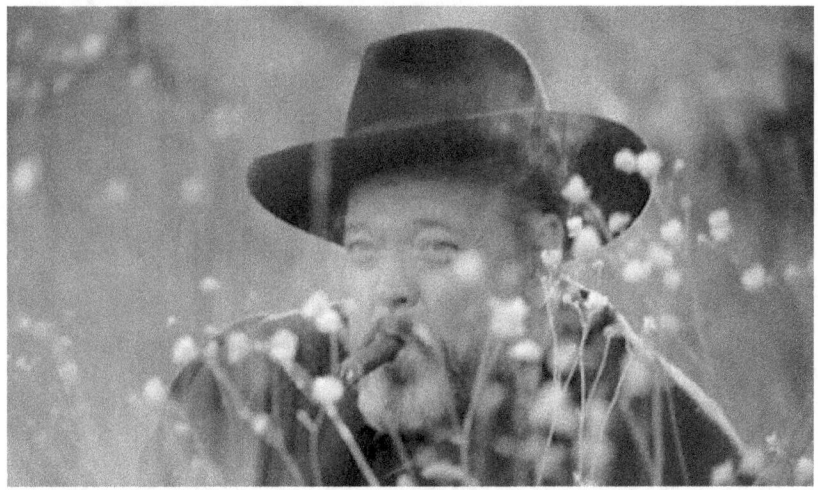

Welles in F For Fake.

Clifford Irving was, of course, the author who wrote the infamous fake autobiography of Howard Hughes, who also wrote the biography of Elmyr the art forger. I spoke with Clifford himself recently about his views on the revolutionary, mind bending film F For Fake, and his place amidst its labyrinthine framework.

"In 1968-69 I helped producer Richard Drewett of the BBC and director Francois Reichenbach film a documentary in Ibiza about Elmyr de Hory," Clifford says. "Orson had no involvement whatsoever with the film and had not yet met de Hory. In 1972-73 Reichenbach and Orson cannibalized parts of the BBC film in the making of F For Fake, without my permission. In 1974, when they were caught out, they were forced to pay me a substantial sum for my 1/8 share. In 1973, when I heard that Orson was involved, I was puzzled as to exactly how he could be involved. I didn't even know if it was true."

Welles focuses in on de Hory, but gives himself enough chances to overlay narratives and reams of different thoughts and observations, the film itself feeling like one big hoax we the viewer might be in on one minute, and be totally oblivious to the next. It has that break neck pace of Citizen Kane, the mischievous narration of the likes of Portrait of Gina (the fact you never quite believe Welles 100 percent makes him an engaging but unreliable narrator), and the multi layers of much of his finest work.

Irving recounted to me his meeting with Orson. "Circa Feb-March 1974, by accident, I bumped into Orson in the Polo Lounge of the Beverly Hills Hotel," he says. "We had never met before. He knew my face, he said, because he'd seen it a thousand times on a cutting-room floor [in the making of FFF]. We made a date for breakfast the next day. He didn't show up and I never heard from him again. I thought the first 2/3 of the film ranged from interesting to fascinating. I particularly liked Orson's profound analysis of Chartres and the lovely sight of my monkey grooming me during Reichenbach's interview. I thought the last third of the film about Picasso and the Hungarian girlfriend was silly and inconsequential."

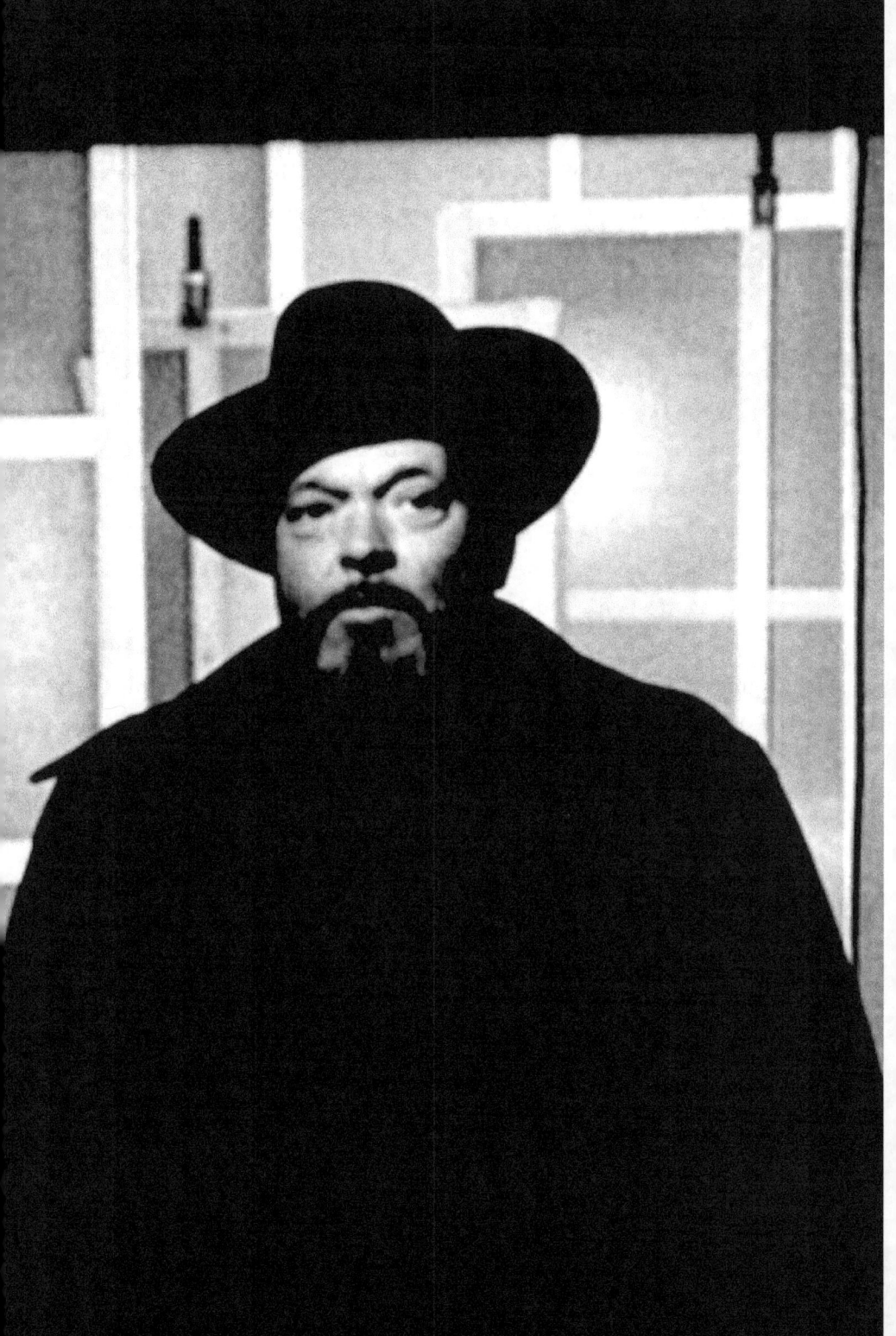

Whether silly and inconsequential or not, it's classic Welles fair, a whirlwind of confusion, charlatanism and illusions, the master of magic pulling out some of his most enigmatic tricks. Not only does it stand alone in Welles' rich and varied canon, but it's a true one off in film history as a whole. What other documentary could concoct a final 20 minutes of film involving Picasso and the director's muse, then turn around and tell us it was all lies?

When Orson tells us at the very start that it's a film about trickery, fraud and lies, we know what kind of a ride we will be in for. Welles knows that as a filmmaker he is in the business of lies (of a sort), but presents these fabricated events in such a manner to entertain and enlighten us. We know as viewers most films are based on fantasies and fabrications, and just because the filmmaker comes on at the start and tells us everything which will follow is based on truth (as indeed Orson does) doesn't mean we should believe them. What should be a dizzying affair, and indeed could have wound up a most frustrating mess, is in fact a film to be in awe of, a dazzling collage of subversive equations and theories.

The film has numerous highlights, but for me one of the most interesting scenes is when Ojar is walking down the street and being ogled, rather unsubtly, by members of the public. This was shot for another project, but Orson includes it in F For Fake, and guides us through the segment. We learn that Welles' camera crew were secretly filming the men's reactions, who were acting away for no pay. He uses the "girl watching" as an example of the film's honesty, and that the movie was made in "blissful ignorance of the facts." This kind of head spinning confusion continues for the whole film and never lets up. Yet somehow, we feel as if we have learned something by the end; not only about perceptions and views (which depend upon where you are standing), but also the human need to befuddle, trick and deceive.

One could immediately say how much Welles was influenced by surrealism, early Dadism and the European cinema of the 50s and 60s, but you could also focus on just how influential this film has been on the generations following its release. The editing alone should be held up as revolutionary. But it is also in its questioning and considerations where the film comes into its own; in its criticisms of the art world, the snobbery, the difference in monetary value between a piece done by a renowned artist and a "non-name", even though they are of equal aesthetic value.

At the time, F For Fake was met with much criticism, a lot of it negative. Clearly, the film was just a few decades ahead of its time. Even now, its release would no doubt trigger confusion, but forty years on, at least Welles' vision is appreciated. It is a movie of illusion, trickery, trust and the feeling you've been had. One is hypnotised by the whizzing cameras, the narration, the multiple viewpoints and approaches to the subjects in question. As an example of Orson Welles as genius, it's certainly up there with Citizen Kane as a prime exhibit.

Though there was a lot of hostility, Roger Ebert was impressed in his review at the time, but he couldn't help but draw parallels to earlier Welles works. "Citizen Kane, for example, is a film so brilliantly packed full of special effects, deceptive shots, double exposures, trick lighting, background animation and back projection that perhaps only a third of the film actually records what we think we're seeing. In F For Fake, Welles plays with the film more obviously, presiding over a ghostly editing room, running shots back and forth in the movieola as he invites us to take a closer look (pick a look, any look...). F For Fake is minor Welles, the master idly tuning his instrument while the concert seems never to start again. But it's engaging and fun, and it's astonishing how easily Welles spins a movie out of next to nothing. For many years, he was reported to have Don Quixote as a work in progress. Now, according to the program notes, the working title has been changed to When Are You Finishing Don Quixote? Does it matter, when F For Fake has such a sufficiency of windmills?"

The point is, you need not compare F For Fake to anything else in the Welles canon. It is, essentially, the last great movie he made, as well as literally the last film he made as the helmer. He was filming and piecing together other projects at the time, but F For Fake remains his last semi fiction directorial swansong. A masterpiece in every sense, a totally immersing experience from its first whirling frame to its last.

Orson Gets the Last Laugh

"It's all right to borrow from others, but what we must never do is borrow from ourselves..."

When receiving his Lifetime Achievement Award from the AFI in 1975, shortly after the muted release of F For Fake, Orson was sure to tell the gathered celebs and ass kissers that he was anything but a spent force. During the night and his inspiring speech, he projected scenes from The Other Side of the Wind, the latest film project

106

taking up most of his time, as if to prove that his upcoming work meant as much to him as the classics meant to them. He drew a line between him and the industry, while also being polite and appreciative of the award at the same time.

"A maverick may go his own way but he doesn't think that it's the only way or ever claim that it's the best one, except maybe for himself," Orson said. "And don't imagine that this raggle-taggle gypsy is claiming to be free. It's just that some of the necessities to which I am a slave are different from yours. As a director, for instance, I pay myself out of my acting jobs. I use my own work to subsidize my work. In other words, I'm crazy. But not crazy enough to pretend to be free. But it's a fact that many of the films you've seen tonight could never have been made otherwise. Or if otherwise, well, they might have been better. But certainly they wouldn't have been mine. The truth is I don't believe that this great evening would ever have brightened my life if it weren't for this, my own particular contrariety. Let us raise our cups then standing, as some of us do, on opposite ends of the river and drink together to what really matters to us all, to our crazy and beloved profession. To the movies, to good movies, to every possible kind. I leave you now in default of the eloquence this high occasion deserves with another very short scene from the same film (Other Side of the Wind) a piece of which you saw earlier with John Huston and Peter Bogdanovich, just by way of saying goodnight from one who will remember tonight, not as a sort of gala visit but as a very happy homecoming. And who remains not only your obedient servant, but also in this age of supermarkets your friendly neighborhood grocery store. The scene that you're going to see takes place in a projection room. And waiting there is the capitol

'B' big studio boss, who is played by Geoffrey Land. And Norman Foster is one of Jake Hannaford's stooges. Jake is the character John Huston plays and he is called Jake because ever since Frank Sinatra and I became friends, he has always called me "Jake." He's the only one who calls me Jake, it's a private joke, and for that reason, this director, who isn't me, is called Jake. Anyway, he has a stooge, and the stooge is trying to sell the unfinished movie that Jake is making, for which he needs end money (laughter). Billy is supposed to explain the plot, as far as he can remember it, and incidentally to sell the movie to Mr. Big, who is a handsome young studio head, a former actor, who by the way bears no resemblance to anyone unless you insist! Thank you and goodnight."

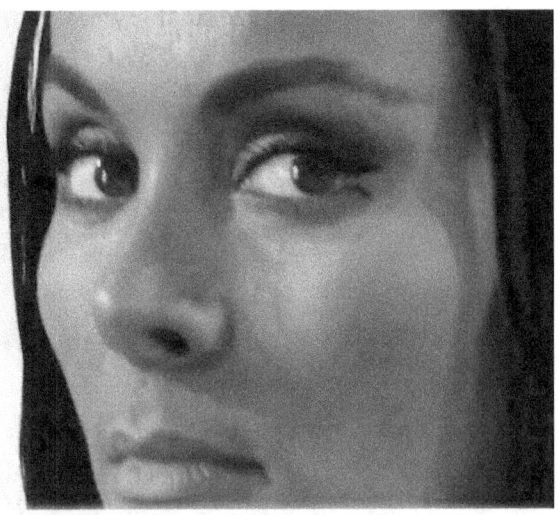

The striking Oja Kodar in the Other Side of the Wind.

Welles knew that the scenes he was projecting for the gathered industry folk were a spoof of the world they lived in (the producer he

108

referred to was, of course, Robert Evans), and his decision to focus on his current project was a wonderful way of reminding them he was not a man of the past. In an earlier interview, he had been asked by Dick Cavett whether Citizen Kane was the greatest film ever made. No, Orson said, that was his next film. Cavett asked what the next film was going to be about, and Welles admitted he had no idea yet. Importantly though, he was always looking forward, onwards towards the future, and believed very much that his true masterpiece was ahead of him, waiting around a corner patiently. That film, in Orson's mind, was no doubt The Other Side of the Wind. But that film would later elude him at every turn, a magical illusion he was unable to decipher.

The birth of the film has been written about repeatedly over the years, sometimes in tireless, though rarely tiring, detail. Yet it is still important to establish the roots of the project and how it began, before diving in to look at the newly released final product, however closely it truly resembles Orson's original aims.

It all began when Ernest Hemingway killed himself in 1961. Famously, a tale often recalled by Welles in later life, Orson and Ernest had a fist fight during a disagreement in the voice over recording of Hemingway's 1937 documentary, The Spanish Earth. The pair were attacking each other with chairs when they suddenly realised how daft the whole thing was, opened a bottle of whiskey and became firm friends from then on. However, upon the legendary writer's death, an idea sparked off in Welles' head. He came up with a screenplay centring on an ageing male, a lover of bullfights and all things macho (like Hemingway, who wrote the essential book on bullfighting), who falls for a young matador. This script fell by the wayside but by the mid 1960s it resurfaced, this time slightly altered, with the bullfight fan now a filmmaker. Still, the theme of suppressed homosexuality, masked beneath a macho mask, remained there in the script.

"Our story is about a pseudo-Hemingway," Welles said at the time, "a movie director. So the central figure... you can barely see through the hair on his chest. He's a movie director who has killed three or four extras on every picture, but is full of charm. Everybody thinks he's great. In our story he's riding around following a bullfighter, and living through him, but he's become obsessed by this young man who has become, his own dream of himself. He's been rejected by all his old friends. He's finally been shown up to be a kind of voyeur, a fellow who lives off other people's danger and death..."

Welles was becoming more serious about the project as the 1960s went on. He had other film projects ready to advance upon, but this one, inspired by a fallen comrade, was taking up most of his attention. Welles was sure the structure and style would be something out of the ordinary, if not completely new. Welles also mentioned at one point that perhaps the making of the movie, or even just the talking about it, was not only more interesting than the movie itself, but actually *was* the movie. "That's how free this is going to be," he said to a potential investor.

"I'm going to use several voices to tell the story," Welles told his friend Bogdanovich. "You hear conversations taped as interviews, and you see quite different scenes going on at the same time. People are writing a book about him—different books. Documentaries, still pictures, films, tapes. All these witnesses. The movie's going to be made up of all this raw material. You can imagine how daring the

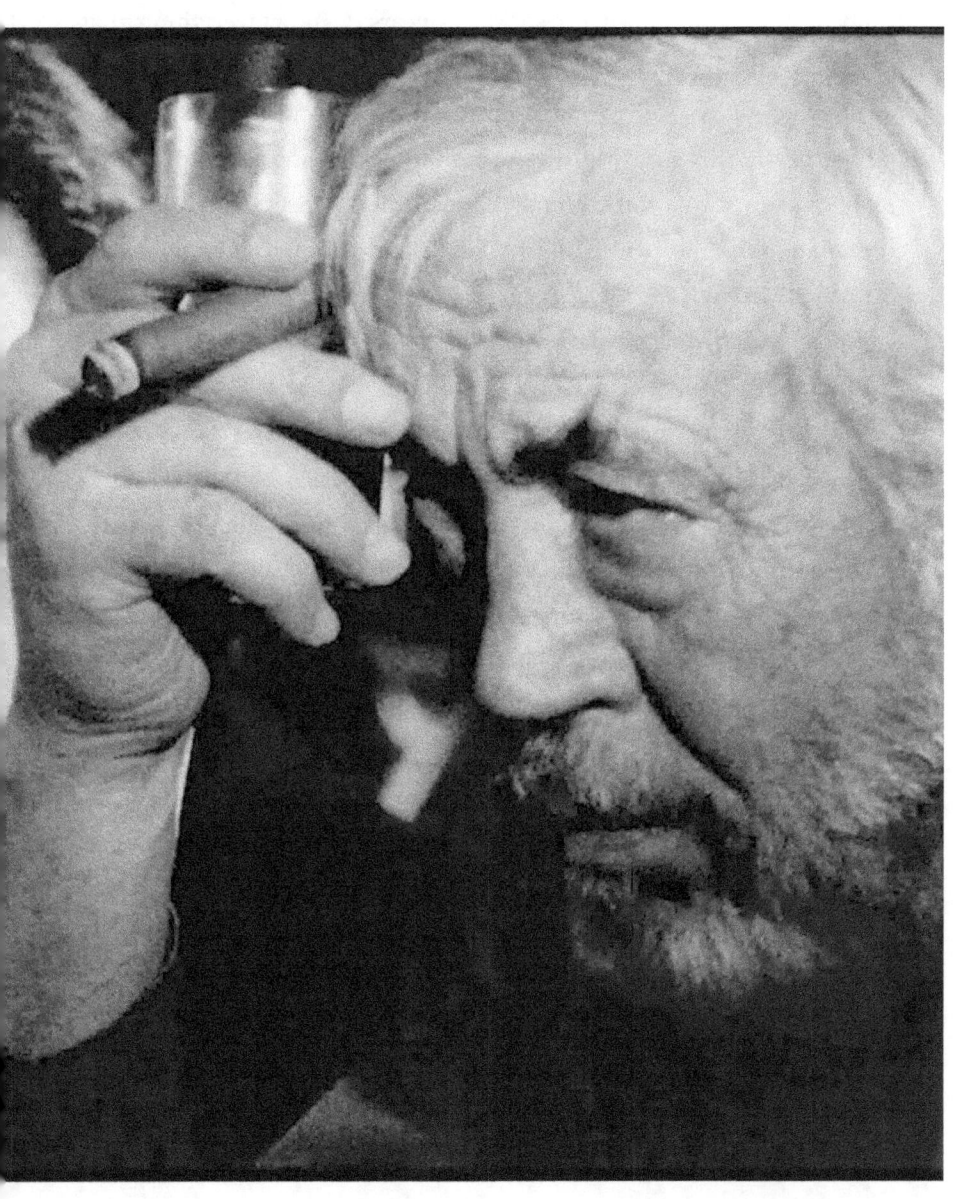

John Huston in Orson Welles' The Other Side of the Wind.

cutting can be, and how much fun. But most of it's got to be ad-libbed. I've worked on it for so long - years. I know everything that happened to that man. I love this man and I hate him." Already, Welles' script was mirroring reality. The "different" books he spoke about in the film's script bring to mind the two books being written about Orson at that time; one by Bogdanovich himself, yet to become the man of the moment with The Last Picture Show and its follow up movies, and the other by Joseph McBride, a young film writer who Orson had invited not only to let him interview him for his forthcoming Welles tome, but also feature in his much spoken of film project. This mythical film director, Jake Hannaford, the centre of his forthcoming picture, was a man worshipped by cineastes and critics, but whose past was more interesting to them than his future. Hannaford, Welles said, simply had to be played by John Huston, the most macho of film directors, and if he couldn't get Huston, Welles was the second man for the job. Later, when Huston had signed up and filming had begun, Welles regretted not giving such a great part to himself.

The first parts of the movie Welles shot were the afore mentioned film within the film, starring his exotic and striking girlfriend Oja Kodar, real name Olga Palinkas (he nicknamed her Oja, the word for "gift" in Croatian). He had met the beauty in the early sixties, pursued her romantically despite being married to Paola Mori, and when she proved resistant to his advances, Orson kicked down her door and hand delivered a love note. From then on the pair were an item. Welles lived a double life as a married man and father to young Beatrice, and as a bohemian artist with Oja, shooting self funded film projects and jet setting across the globe with his camera. Welles somehow kept up the illusion until 1984, living with his family in Las Vegas and in Hollywood with Oja, though it's doubtful Paola was not aware of their affair.

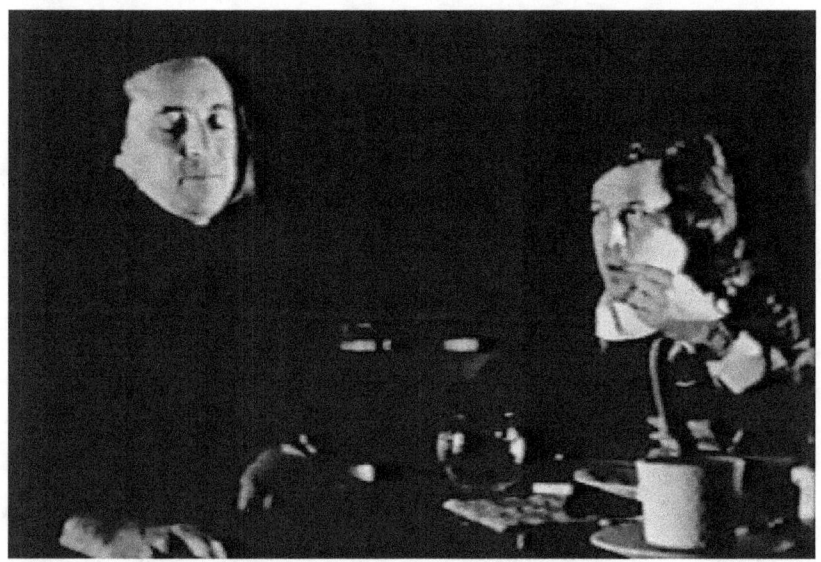

In the purposely arty and pretentious film within the film, a clear spoof of European greats of the moment like Michelangelo Antonioni, the young actor Bob Random pursues Oja through various odd scenarios, famously romping with her in a moving car (though it wasn't actually moving, just being rocked by Welles' helpers) and then on a rusty bed in an obscure setting. Anyone seeing these clips independently from the whole of the movie might be forgiven for thinking Welles had disappeared up his own rectum. But Welles admitted he was doing these scenes in a typical arty style for the day, and found it liberating to work on footage that was in itself very un-Wellesian.

"There were no discussions of motivations or psychology and no script that I ever saw," Bob Random recalled to the brilliant Wellesnet website. "Just situations with Orson coaching directions off-camera – and often laughing out loud. All the footage of Oja and me was shot MOS [without sound]. He had a good time and so did I. All of my footage was shot from early September to late December in 1970. Working for Orson was a dream; for one thing, he was Orson! Yes, he was very patient and considerate of the cast but every now and then he could get exasperated. In the heat of the moment he occasionally went off on the crew for some failure to communicate but it was short-lived and evaporated quickly. A couple of times he even apologised. The small crew of young film enthusiasts were dedicated and savvy so they just let him vent."

"There's a film with the film, which I made with my own money," Welles recalled. "It's the old man's attempt to do a kind of counterculture film, in a surrealist, dreamlike style. We see some of it in the director's projection room, some of it at a drive-in when that breaks down. It's about 50% of the whole movie. Not the kind of film I'd want to make; I've invented a style for him."

Welles also filmed some of the "party" footage in early stages. The film would be focusing on the last day of Hannaford's life, his 70th birthday in fact, where filmmakers, cineastes, old friends and hangers on were gathered in a lavish home for celebrations. Welles shot some footage with filmmakers Henry Jaglom and Paul Mazursky, sitting off camera in character as Hannaford, all this before Huston had been cast. Putting two rising young New Hollywood filmmakers against each other (Mazurksy the director of a recent hit, Jaglom the art house avant-garde director on the side lines), he delighted in combining fact with fiction, and watching the friction increase between the two men, Jaglom goading Mazurksy on and derogatorily referring to his selling out. The raw footage has been available for some time, but unfortunately is missing from the newly released cut save for a small fragment.

"Orson and I were doing a number on Mazursky, who had no idea what was going on, which worked perfectly toward Orson's purposes. We planned it out completely. He wanted me to imply Hannaford's ultra-masculinity (like Hemingway, Orson's model for the role) was hiding a homosexual discomfort. So sorry Peter cut that all out of the finished film..."

Filming ceased abruptly in 1971 when Orson was faced with some serious tax issues, and had to work on other projects to pay the bills. By 1973, Welles had raised more funds, including some from France and Iran, and more footage was shot, considering of course who was available and willing to work at the time. Most of the party footage was shot in 1974, with Huston as Hannaford at Southwestern Studio in Arizona, with a rented mansion doubling as the living room set. The gathered actors, writers and misfits were still unaware of how the film would hold together, if it would at all in fact, but went along with whatever Orson suggested out of sheer belief and love. Orson was the maestro and they would have jumped off a cliff if he'd requested they do so.

As the project went on, and Peter Bogdanovich had established himself as New Hollywood's leading light (or one of them at least), Orson no longer could afford the studio and mansion to film his party scenes. Out of kindness, Peter let Orson stay in his house and film sections there. He may have out stayed his welcome (he was there for two years), but Peter didn't complain. Naturally of course, Peter was hurt when Welles and Burt Reynolds later insulted him on a chat show pilot, which seemed unfair given how kind he had been to Orson in the mid seventies.

Hilariously, and rather sadly given Welles' stature today, the scenes shot at MGM's studios were done without consent of the film company. The crew pretended to be film students and snuck Welles inside in a darkened van, where the scenes were finished as speedily as possible before the studio staff noticed. Orson, recognisable to most people in the world at that time, had to duck when they passed security at the gate.

It was in 1974 that the real serious problems began. Financial and investment issues basically spelled the end of production, and any work that did continue from here on in was done slowly and with much difficulty. After his AFI speech drew no backers, and he began to experience friction with the Iranian management company who owned a stake in the picture, Welles was only able to edit the film as and when he could in his spare time. By the late 70s Welles had 40 minutes of it completed, but legal problems heightened to the stage that ownership complications resulted in the film being sent off to a vault in Paris.

"Many times it seemed he's get the funds," Henry tells me. "We went to Paris and testified at a trial and created a company, WELJAG, to do it, but it never came to be."

After Orson died, it looked like any hope of the film being released died with him. Despite attempts to revive it in the late 90s, nobody could agree on the terms. Beatrice Welles was the first to end a deal with Showtime, who had promised to provide end money for the movie. Oja Kodar had been left the rights to a lot of Welles footage and she too had a say in the fate of The Other Side of the Wind. For years all we had, thanks to Welles' loyal cinematographer Gary Graver, were a few reels of crackly footage, basically rough edits of a few sequences, and it looked like that was all we were ever going to get.

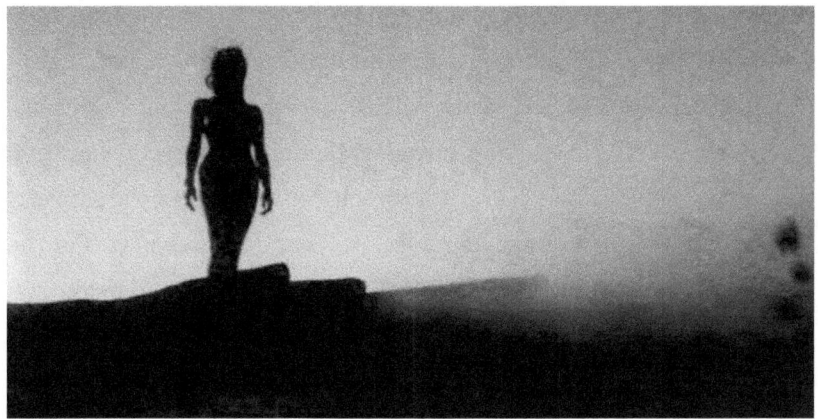

Other attempts to get the film made were aborted by Oja, who was asking for a high price to give up her rights. By 2014, the film was looking like a reality, thanks to Frank Marshall, and when an Indiegogo launch raised a further million, Netflix stepped in to hand over the much needed 5 million to finish it.

In November of 2018, it miraculously appeared, unbelievably, on Netflix, viewable on TV screens, computers, laptops, tablets and even phones for a viewing. We had been waiting for this moment for so long (some had been waiting decades), and here it was, the legendary film which had eluded so many people and always seemed just out of reach. I have to confess I felt a little reluctant to watch it. Why? Was it because I feared being disappointed? Or was it more to do with the film's myth, that once I saw it I would no longer be waiting to see it, wondering what it was like, and speculating about its labyrinthine mystery. In the end, I built up the courage, turned down the lights and transported myself off to Welles' magical world.

Thankfully, within minutes I realised it was not going to be a disappointment, and in its chaotic, swirling madness, the film more than stood up to its own legend. Beginning with Peter Bogdanovich's voice over, in character as Hannaford's protégé filmmaker Brooks Otterlake, the film opens up to reveal the fact Hannaford (Huston) died in a car crash in his 70th birthday. Before his death he had been trying to get with the New Hollywood crowd, making a sexually provocative art film aimed to appeal to younger audiences. On the day of the party, it is clear the film has been left abandoned, with Hollywood producer Max David viewing sections from the patchy work in progress, of which filming was cut short when the lead actor stormed off set, for reasons later revealed to us all.

As pretentious and purposely self conscious the film within a film is supposed to be, it's actually very enjoyable, deliciously surreal and high on atmosphere and sexual tension. Kodar, though playing a Euro film goddess parody, is magnetic on screen and one can not keep ones' eyes off her. Though you do get the feeling that Welles is proudly displaying his striking lover for the world to see - and every bit of her, quite literally - you cannot deny her power and sensuality.

Orson's son Christopher once said that there was only woman who could control Orson and make him do as she wished, and that was Oja. With other women, Orson was the boss; with Oja, it was very much a partnership, though one might say Oja could wrap dear Orson around her little finger. And it's not as if Oja was some empty beauty, easy on the eye but with little else to offer; she was and still is a strong woman with her own mind and ideas. Though we are

118

supposed to roll our eyes at the surrealistic sequences within the film, these segments are utterly bewitching.

As the party goes on, Hannaford gets drunker and drunker, and characters who firstly seem like mere caricatures of Hollywood types reveal themselves to be parodies of well known figures from Welles folk lore. Indeed, one might have to be familiar with the Welles myth and history to fully appreciate what's going on throughout the party. It was comedian Rich Little who first took on the role of Brooks Otterlake, a former Hannaford (or should that be Welles) disciple and worshipper who has now become a name in his own right. When Little pulled out due to prior commitments, Bogdanovich stepped in to his shoes, and perhaps then realised that Brooks Otterlake was a spoof on himself, that former film writer who was now a Hollywood big shot, with blonde actress wife (Cybil Shepherd) and a mansion of his own.

Representatives of the New Hollywood movement, who so adored Welles, include Dennis Hopper, whose rambling speeches are cut down to a small number of observations in the finished cut, alongside Jaglom and Mazursky. Only Jaglom had serious ties to Welles; he had just directed him in his first picture, A Safe Place, and would not only collaborate with him again at the end of his life, but also become a firm friend and unofficial agent and funds seeker. His presence, though brief, is rather comforting.

Hannaford himself, a man's man never without a whiskey in his hand, might be modelled on the macho Hemingway, but in his towering reputation and with fawning ass kissers on his tail at all times, he is clearly a warped version of Welles. Susan Strasberg, cast as Juliette Rich, a film critic always trying to define Hannaford to within an inch of his life, is clearly modelled on an old Welles nemesis, the savage Pauline Kael, who famously damned Welles in her appalling film essay, Raising Kane, in which she claimed Orson was not the man responsible for Citizen Kane's greatness. Then there is Lilli Palmer, who plays a kind of Marlene Dietrich parody (though a sympathetic one), and perhaps funniest of all Geoffrey land as the Robert Evans spoof Max David.

Much of the film concerns Hannaford's sparring with various friends and foes, all of whom he chooses to see as obstacles, and the tension mounting towards the climax of the party, where we may learn why the star of his film stormed off the set. The party scenes are so frantic and frenetic in their editing that without the more calm, subdued and genuinely enjoyable Oja Kodar moments, the whole thing could have become exhausting. As they are though, the film within the film elements offer the viewer a chance to have a breather, and simply enjoy Hannaford's attempts to fit in with modern tastes; or more fittingly, Welles' knack of not only spoofing but equalling, in atmosphere alone at least, the European masters of the day. One cannot deny Huston's performance is naturalistically engaging (he is tirelessly brilliant), but the film as a whole, with its vastly contrasting shades, is what the viewer should come away with. In fact, the film is such a result of collaboration between cast and crew that even though Welles is clearly the mastermind behind it all, one cannot help but come away with the feeling that every element, every cast member, even every frame is equally vital to the success of the picture.

The party scenes are certainly similar, in cutting, editing and tone, to the contradictory magic of F For Fake, Welles' 1973 film essay masterpiece, but in their jumpy jerkiness are like nothing else I have ever seen before. Even in death, it seems Welles has created another new genre, a realist fantasy from endless, multiple angles, cut rapidly, jarringly at times, coming from the most unlikely of viewpoints, with dialogue overlapping, faces appearing from nowhere and activity non stop. Though tireless, it is never tiring, but that could be more down to the mercifully slower fantastical film within the film sequences than anything within the main party scenes.

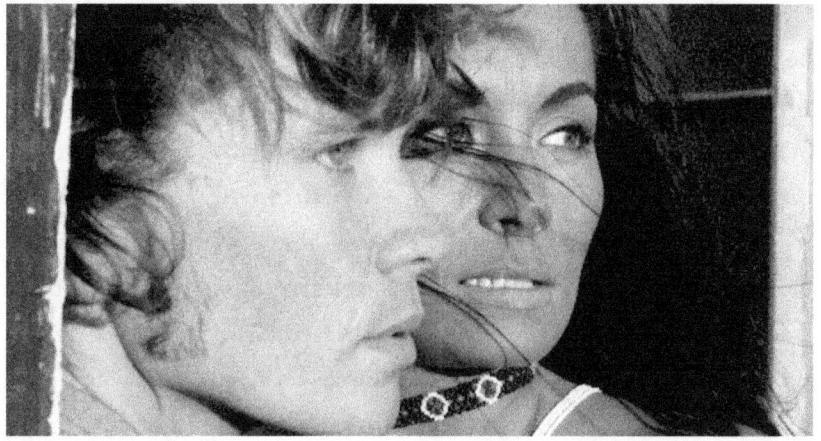

Welles had edited around a third of the film, meaning it was up to Frank Marshall and Peter Bogdanovich to ensure that the remaining two thirds or so would be loyal to Orson's vision, or as much was possible at least. Referring to his notes, compiling all audio and visual material, they set to work, with Editor Bob Murawski, to help complete the rest. No doubt Orson, if he were able to see the film, would shake his head and write a list of possible corrections. But one cannot help but feel he would be proud. There is also the idea that Welles would simply love the chaotic irony of it all. In life, he could not even get enough funds to finish the damn thing. In his death, there was internet crowd funding, shipments of film reels sent across the world, years of hard work, tons of speculation and media interest, multi million dollar deals, and the whole world of film lovers waiting with bated breath for his final statement.

When watching the film, one certainly feels the presence of Orson. Though Welles may not be in the film, he is definitely there, and it's the image of him off to one side, smiling, revelling in the cyclonic chaos, that makes the film all the more effective. This isn't just Orson's last picture, but Orson's last laugh too. While I genuinely believe he wanted the film to be completed (regardless of daft rumours going around that the last thing he wanted was The Other Side of the Wind to be finished) I also believe he purposely engineered the film to not enhance his own myth, but to become a myth in itself. In many ways, the making of and the very idea of The Other Side of the Wind is more fascinating, or at least as equally fascinating, as the film we have been presented with today. There is no doubt that the movie is brilliant, a masterpiece which at its centre features a characters worthy to rival Charles Foster Kane in enigma and complications, but it is also brilliant as an observation, a statement about the film world and the myths attached to it.

"I wish they'd kept all my stuff in," Jaglom told me, "especially as it was focused on the implied homosexuality of the director's relationships with his male stars. Peter told me that they couldn't use it because the off-camera responses of Hanford (John Huston) had never been shot, but I don't agree that they would have been necessary. But that was Peter's choice and I think on the whole he did a fantastic job."

I also asked Henry what he thought about the film finally coming out. "I was excited and hopeful but reluctantly suspicious because I knew all the stuff he hadn't managed to shoot" After watching it, Jaglom shared his thoughts with me:

"I'm excited by it, especially the first hour, because I see where he was going. But I'm saddened by the second half, because it reveals the sad fact that he never competed it and it therefore just stages his material out by repetition, things he never would have left in, like the 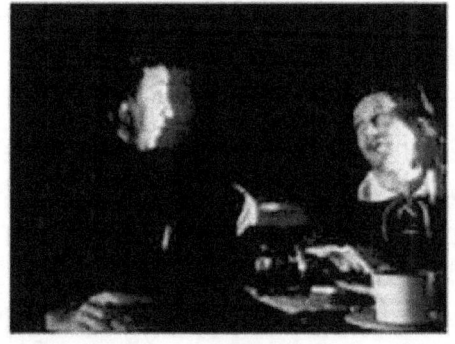 endless scenes of Oja walking and walking naked in the movie within the movie; though he was making fun of the then new (70s) sex stuff in movies, he never would have left all the repetitiousness of the second half in a film of his, had he been able to finish it. Still, it's very exciting to see what he was going for; I just wish he had had the ability to finish it. If it were it up to me I would have left it much shorter, as he would have using only the material he had..."

Hannaford, for my money, belongs and fits in firmly with Welles' most legendary figures. He has the charisma and power, marred by the sexism, alcoholism and questionable leery qualities. (Notice the youthfulness of his girlfriend.) The final joke of course, is the suggestion that Hannaford is actually a closet homosexual in love with his male star, who he humiliates during filming with off screen

123

orders and degrading requests through a megaphone. Anyone aware of Welles and Hemingway's brief spat will know that Orson wound Hemingway up by feigning campness (Hemingway later said that Welles sounded like a "cocksucker" during narration for the Spanish Earth), suggesting the ultra macho writer was in fact secretly gay. Again, Orson has the last laugh.

That said, Orson reveals his own suppressed vulnerabilities too; Hannaford's relationship with Otterlake, oh so close to his and Bogdanovich's, hints at the complexities of that friendship. In many ways, at the start, Orson was the master and Peter the hungry cineaste, massaging Welles' ego while working on their book. Fast forward a mere two or three years and Peter was the "it" guy of Hollywood, Welles a yesterday man, lauded for a work that was three decades old, with Peter as hot box office golden boy. It was as if Orson needed him more than Peter needed Orson. (How smugly glad Orson seemed to be when Peter's career began to decline.)

The only problem with the film is whether Orson really wanted the whole film edited in the vein he had put together his own 45 minutes of film. Bob Murawski, a gifted editor of course, has done a brilliant job in replicating the speedy frenzy of Orson's completed footage. The question is of course, did Orson intend the whole film to be quite so chaotic? One can only presume so. Credit must also go to the sound mixer, Scott Milan, in tidying up the often muffled, messy audio and arranging actors to do sound-alike overdubs when dialogue was inaudible. The icing on the cake, and the final Wellesian element to give it true authenticity, is the musical score, written by F For Fake composer Michel Legrand. Both the classical and jazz arrangements establish the era perfectly, the transitional phase between both the Old and the New Hollywood.

It seems odd that such a monumental film with so much mythical history attached to it should just drop one Friday on to a streaming service. The film did have a cinematic premier and is being shown around the world at selected theatres as I write this piece, but there is a sharp irony in the fact that something that was once so unobtainable is now available for every one in the world, at their finger tips, waiting for them to see it. It's an irony I am sure Orson Welles himself would have been delighted by.

So far, reactions have been positive, especially from Orson fans, many of whom hail it as a masterpiece and essential final chapter in the great man's cinematic journey. Even those critical of it as a finished product (what a terrible word to use) are still impressed by its ambition and worth, even if only as a posthumous final kick in the balls from Orson, a last defiant cry against a Hollywood that chewed him up and spat him out. Most reviews admired it, though few said it could ever equal Citizen Kane. Perhaps the strangest comment from reviewers is that "it isn't for everyone." Tell me then, just what is...

Peter Travers, writing for Rolling Stone, gave the film 4 out of 5, stating: "What to call this Hollywood takedown from Orson Welles, besides the best 1970's movie to be released in the 21st century? Welles scholars will be in nirvana, savouring every detail about the final film from the former boy wonder who gave the world *Citizen Kane*. There are times in Wind when Welles seems to be settling scores, showing Jake swimming with sharks and barely surviving under an annihilating Tinseltown glare. In his filmmaking technique, Welles is miles from the deep focus elegance of Kane, The

Magnificent Ambersons and Touch of Evil. Using quick cuts and fragments of scenes shot on the go by cinematographer Gary Graver, the movie renders the chaos of a Hollywood imploding from its own hubris. That's the same industry that left Welles adrift at the end of his career. So to answer the question posed at the start of this review, the chaotic, jumbled The Other Side of the Wind isn't for everyone — just folks who cares about the history of film and the master builder who helped make it great."

Peter Bradshaw of the Guardian called it a hurricane of anger and wit: "There are references to Fellini here, with the surreal appearance of dwarves, but the comparison is misleading. The Other Side of the Wind really looks more like an experimental American movie of that time. It resembles The Last Movie by Dennis Hopper (who has a cameo here) or the early, scrappy pictures of Brian De Palma: Hi Mom! and Greetings. It is a vivid snapshot of a turbulent zeitgeist, the ordeal of making a film independently, the agony of feeling oneself obsolete. Watching The Other Side of the Wind, I found myself thinking of the final scene in David Niven's Hollywood memoir, The Moon's A Balloon, in which he remembers turning up to a trendy Hollywood party and being harangued by a aggressive hippy-ish guy for being irrelevant, but then told he could atone for his sins by coming up with some "heavy bread" for this man's new film company. Niven seraphically accepts that his time is up. But Welles is angry: rage and frustration punch holes in this film. Whatever its flaws, it is an enthralling portrait and a study of work destined always to be in progress."

Personally, I can obviously see how someone who has only previously seen Kane from Orson's filmography might be in a constant state of shock when viewing The Other Side of the Wind, but for me it is the essential counterpart to that iconic, perfect movie, "the Greatest Film Ever Made" no less. Though obviously nothing Welles made after could nab its mighty title at the very zenith of filmmaking, The Other Side of the Wind is like Kane turned upside down, the fantastical magic tossed aside to reveal the rot within, the truth of Hollywood and how it feels to be yesterday's news, despite having more energy, life and ideas in you than ten young men. The film then, often feels like a snarl, a biting of the hand that refuses to feed but pats you on the head in acknowledgement for past glories.

Do I feel it's a great film? Definitely, as much as my humble opinion matters in a mass sea of overlapping voices, each one as smugly opinionated as the next, just like the hangers on and parasites following Hannaford in The Other Side of the Wind, applauding, crawling, yet sneering when his back is turned. This monumental film, arriving decades after the death of one of cinema's true titans, is a cause for celebration, and it should be treated as the event it is. I feel it's an important work about the film world, the hypocrisy and bare faced cheek of an industry so up itself it doesn't know which way to pontificate out of. I feel it will be dissected and written about for years to come. And who knows, one day it might even be accepted as the long lost mutant brother of Citizen Kane.

To assess Kane and Wind properly as the start and end of a life in movies, it is essential to look at the 70 odd years that separate them as released films. Orson's directorial career was a journey, an adventure of myth, full of ups, downs and endless frustrations. Given Welles' often torturous quest for funds and artistic freedom, The Other Side of the Wind is cathartic in its sense of release, the way it brings the spirit of Orson back amongst us. In a tidal wave of blockbusters, crowd pleasers, robo-actioners and sci-fi soap operas, The Other Side of the Wind stands as a brave experiment in filmmaking. It almost feels like Orson is alive and amongst us once again. And in a funny way, he is.

ABOUT CHRIS WADE

Chris Wade is a UK based writer, filmmaker and musician. As well as running the acclaimed music project Dodson and Fogg, he has written books on The Kinks, Malcolm McDowell, Captain Beefheart, Robert De Niro and many others. He has also released audiobooks of his comedic fiction, such as Cutey and the Sofaguard, narrated by Rik Mayall. His other projects include Rainsmoke, a musical outfit with actor Nigel Planer, and Hound Dawg Magazine, for which he has interviewed such people as Sharon Stone, Donovan and Jethro Tull's Ian Anderson. His art films include The Apple Picker (accepted by Sydney World Film Festival, featuring Toyah Willcox and Nigel Planer), and he also made a documentary on jazz singing Surrealist George Melly.

More info at his website: wisdomtwinsbooks.weebly.com

www.ingramcontent.com/pod-product-compliance
Lightning Source LLC
Chambersburg PA
CBHW071447180526
45170CB00001B/493